THE COMPLETE BOOK
OF NASCAR
STOCK CAR RACING

THE COMPLETE BOOK OF NASCAR STOCK CAR RACING

Produced by Lyle Kenyon Engel

in association with the Editorial Staff
of *Auto Racing* magazine

Revised Edition

Editorial Staff:
Bob Glendy
Marla Ray
George Engel

FOUR WINDS PRESS
NEW YORK

Library of Congress Cataloging in Publication Data
Engel, Lyle Kenyon.
The complete book of NASCAR stock car racing.
1. National Association for Stock Car Racing.
I. Auto Racing.   II. Title.
GV1029.E5 1974   796.7'2'0973   74–5112
ISBN 0–590–07396–6

All photos courtesy of
Auto Racing magazine

Published by Four Winds Press
A Division of Scholastic Magazines, Inc., New York, New York
Copyright © 1974, 1968 by Lyle Kenyon Engel
All rights reserved
Printed in the United States of America
Library of Congress Catalog Card Number: 74–5112
1   2   3   4   5   78   77   76   75   74

7

THE WESTERN GRAND NATIONAL DIVISION

8

THE PAVED SUPERSPEEDWAYS

THE COMPLETE BOOK
OF NASCAR
STOCK CAR RACING

INTRODUCTION

by William H. G. (Bill) France
President of NASCAR and International Speedway Corporation

William H. G. (Bill) France is president of the world's largest stock car racing organization (NASCAR) and the world's fastest speedway (Alabama International Speedway). He is "Mr. Racing" in the United States. His experience as driver, mechanic, car owner, organizer and official not only influenced the growth of stock car racing in this country, but also was of great help in the guidance of international motor sports. It was Bill France who revived racing on the famous old beach and road course at Daytona, Florida, masterminded the formation of NASCAR and guided the organization to the international esteem it enjoys today.

Man's never-ending quest for excellence, which has led to almost unbelievable records in all fields of endeavor, is no better exemplified than in motor sports. The body of man may have its limits but the mind of man is boundless. Mechanical ingenuity has combined with physical stamina and the magnificent bravery of drivers to make motor sports goals limitless.

It's been that way since the first engine turned the first wheel: Someone always finds a way to make the wheels turn faster, and there is a seemingly endless list of men brave enough to drive automobiles to the ragged edge and sometimes beyond. The popularity of stock car racing was inevitable. The motor sports fan enjoyed the superspeeds of the exotic, specially built machines of the olden days, but it was the thought of his family car being a little stronger than his neighbor's that really turned him on.

In the beginning stock car racing had no direction. Drivers entered the cars they drove to the track, making only minor changes and adjustments for safety. While the need for direction was always there, it was not until stock car racing was resumed following World War II, with bigger and faster cars than ever, that sensible men decided that by banding together the sport could gain the prominence it deserved. The National Association for Stock Car Automobile

7

Racing (NASCAR) was formed in February, 1948.

In the past 26 years stock car racing has grown into a highly competitive, highly respected sport followed avidly by people from all walks of life. From a humble beginning (there were 875 members in 1949) NASCAR has become the world's leading stock car racing organization with a membership in excess of 16,000 and over 90 sanctioned race tracks. NASCAR sanctions more than 1,600 events each year with prize money totaling more than $5,000,000. There were more than 7,000,000 spectators at NASCAR events in 1971. Stock car racing has spurred the growth of motor sports popularity to the point that auto racing is now the No. 2 spectator sport in the United States, second only to horse racing. It is No. 1 among sports without pari-mutuel betting.

While I look proudly at the enormous interest in our sport today, I am more impressed and pleased by the contributions stock car racing and NASCAR have made in highway safety and engineering advancement. Many safety devices developed in racing and required before a stock car can compete in a NASCAR event are now standard equipment on passenger cars. Manufacturers and agencies request the assistance of NASCAR in various testing programs.

As president of NASCAR, I am deeply grateful to the thousands of drivers, mechanics, car owners and officials who have given so generously of their time and talents to boost stock car racing to the high level of prestige it holds today.

In 1972, Bill France announced his retirement as president of NASCAR, turning the reins of this organization over to his son, William C. France. Bill, Sr. remains as president of the International Speedway Corporation which owns the Daytona and Talladega speedways.

Bill France, Jr.

8

PREFACE

THE WORLD OF STOCK CAR RACING

by David Pearson
NASCAR Grand National Champion

David Pearson is one of only three men ever to win the NASCAR Grand National Point Championship three times. The Spartanburg, South Carolina driver captured the coveted title in 1966, 1968 and again in 1969. Pearson has won more than 60 Grand National races in a career which dates back to 1960. The 1959 South Carolina Sportsman Champion and 1960 NASCAR Rookie of the Year has won more than $700,000. Pearson began his career driving a Pontiac for Ray Fox and has driven Cotton Owens-built Dodges and Holman-Moody Fords. In 1971 Pearson left Holman-Moody to help develop a competitive Pontiac for Chris Vallo and Nichels Engineering.

Stock car racing is two ends of the world. You win and you're at the very top. You're surrounded by fans. You're a great driver and a great guy. You blow an engine, strip a gear, blow a tire and hit the wall or do one of thousands of freakish things that can keep you from victory lane and you're a nobody. You take your busted racer to the garage area and sit in solitude to dream about the next week . . . another race . . . and perhaps a share of glory. There's nothing to compare with stock car racing.

You earn every nickel you make and you deserve every ounce of credit you get. Nothing comes easy. It takes most of what you win, even when you win consistently, to keep on the road from race to race and to keep your car in condition to win—and run again and again. You're away from home 40 weeks out of 52. When you're not driving in a race, you're driving to a race.

While stock car racing has mushroomed in prominence in the past five years, it still does not have the glamour of the Indianapolis "500." There they call drivers "Mister." I don't want to be called "Mister," but I'm looking forward to the day when the stock car

9

racing banner flies high among the professional sports, when a driver who makes the sacrifices to rank among the best can soothe his aching muscles after a 500-lap race with the same percentage of money that goes to boxers, baseball players and golfers.

I'm not griping. I don't think I'd swap stock car racing for anything. The sport has been good to me and my family. And even when it wasn't good, when I came home with less money than I had when I left, I loved every minute of it.

Stock car racing is like a giant carnival—on the move from town to town. Every track is different, and you have to set up your car to meet a new challenge every week. It means hard work for your mechanics—the real heroes of the sport who never get any credit. They work day and night making your car safe and fast. Then they risk their necks in the pits on race day, working with their backs to high-speed traffic to change your tires and give you a tank of gas in 20 seconds. They are in more danger than the driver, who sits harnessed in 4,000 pounds of protective steel and iron.

The sport of stock car racing started on a back street somewhere with a guy matching his family car against a neighbor's. Then someone got the idea of putting the cars on an oval track and running them, just as they came from the showroom.

As the years passed, the people connected with racing evolved safety measures. They were first to use leather straps to make sure doors stayed closed in an accident; later they progressed to bolted doors. They added crash helmets, then seat belts and roll bars. They learned through experience. They equipped their cars with heavy duty suspensions and safety shields for the fuel tanks. The cars became safer—and faster.

The drivers, too, develop and improve. You don't find many who started out at the top. Most are like me, first racing the kid next door, then discovering the race track. I started in an old 1939 Ford coupe purchased for $40.00. And I started on a dimly lit, dirt track. I ate a lot of dirt before I felt I was good enough and got the break that put me in the big-time of stock car racing.

There are a lot of guys out there today, eating the dirt, pushing old worn-out cars and hoping to get the same kind of break. It's not an easy road. The old dirt tracks are not only dusty, they are full of holes and bumpy. They tear up equipment. It keeps you working to keep a car going.

If you're a winner it's tougher than ever. You're like the gunman in a Western movie. You have a reputation, and everyone is after you to see if you're really that good. Some of the small tracks ban the consistent winners, because it hurts the gate to have the same driver win each week. Others will put a bounty on your head—a bonus for the driver who beats you.

I guess it's the ambition of every southern stock car driver to get into the National Association for Stock Car Auto Racing and eventually get a Grand National ride. The big money is in the Grand Nationals—and it is there only for those who have top equipment.

I ran the Late Model Sportsman circuit when I first joined NASCAR, figuring I would get a Late Model sponsor if I did well in Sportsman competition. I entered 42 races and won 30, including the state championship. But nobody came tearing the door down to hire me. So I persuaded my father to help purchase a Late Model race car. With the help of some friends I managed to get a 1959 Chevrolet, one on which Jack Smith had put a lot of racing miles the year before. I found out in a hurry that it takes more than a car and desire to win a race.

I guess the longest day of my life was in the World 600 at Charlotte, North Carolina. It was the first race on the 1½-mile track and the asphalt had not cured properly. We knew it would come out in chunks, and most of the drivers put plastic or screen wire over their windshields.

My car wasn't as fast as most of the factory-sponsored cars, but I hung in there. I was running in the top five at one time when my generator fell off. We wired it back with a coat hanger to finish the race. The track was hot and dirty. After more than five hours I ached in every joint. My hands were covered with blisters. I didn't make enough to pay for the tires I used—much less the damage to the car. You wonder if it's worth it as you nurse your aches and pains. The mere mention of the next race makes you forget such a thought. It's that never-ending challenge.

I went back to Charlotte the next year with the same old car. I hadn't won a race in 1960, but I had done well enough to be named NASCAR Rookie of the Year. That was my first big thrill in racing. Then I had an invitation from Ray Fox to drive his factory-sponsored Pontiac. That's the break it took—the kind of break every young driver (and some older ones, too) hopes for. Most never get it.

I was determined to make good, although I was scared to death that I'd wreck and blow my chances forever. Fireball Roberts, who died of burns suffered on the same track a few years later, did a lot to soothe my nerves. I went out with him the night before the race, and he told me he was really afraid I'd beat him. He gave me a lot of confidence.

11

When the green flag dropped to start the 600 miles, I never once thought about anything but winning. It was just like driving one of the short, dirt track races. It was hot—so hot you could hardly breathe, but you didn't have time to think about that. We couldn't even relax during the extra-long caution flag. Red Cagle had crashed into the second-turn guard rail, and a section of the steel retainer pierced the front of his car and came out the door on the driver's side.

I was leading the race at the time and I didn't look up the bank as we passed the wreck scene. I was afraid he had been killed, and seeing such a horrible accident in a race I was driving was something new. It was not until after the race that I learned he had lost a leg—but miraculously was alive. It didn't make it any easier to drive the rest of that race with a gaping hole in the guard rail reminding us of what could happen if we blew a tire or lost control.

I went on to win the race—my first big victory. I won two other major races that year and was top money winner. It was a good year. I wish they all had been as good. In racing, luck runs in streaks—bad and good. Just as it was all good in 1961, it was all bad in 1962. Mechanical trouble, a slow car spinning out directly in front, tire failures and, I must admit, some driver faults made victory lane seem a long way off. It takes a lot of people and a lot of things working together to make the victory circle.

As I said, I think my career is typical of most—with a few more good breaks tossed in.

For four years I had been associated with Cotton Owens, in my opinion the best all-around mechanic in racing. Cotton was a great driver—and still is for that matter. He's had to give up the steering wheel because of an eye injury suffered in a Modified wreck back in 1952.

He is a perfectionist when it comes to safety. I don't mind that. I hit the fourth-turn concrete wall at Daytona several years ago when a piece of metal on the track ruptured my right front tire. I was running over 170 mph. A precautionary steel brace Cotton had attached to the front frame rail and the top of the roll-bar cage kept the front of the car from crushing back into the cockpit. All I got was a bad seat-belt burn.

This is where I feel I'm lucky—lucky to have a top car owner and mechanic. There are only a few around—men like Cotton, Bud Moore, Lee Petty, Ray Fox, Smokey Yunick, Glen and Leonard Wood, Ray Nichels, John Holman, Ralph Moody and Jack Sullivan. Only about a dozen drivers get the good cars. That means there are a hundred or more struggling to get the big break—the break I got back in 1961.

In the four years I raced cars for Owens we had our ups and downs. I guess the low spot was in 1964 when I hit the wall at Daytona. I set a record for qualifying honors that year but wound up with only nine victories, all on short tracks. I was voted Hard Luck Driver of the Year. It was one of those years when everything went wrong on the big tracks.

In 1965, when the Chrysler hemi was banned from NASCAR, I tried my hand at drag racing, the Pikes Peak Hill Climb, sports car racing and even took a ride in an Indy car during tests at Atlanta, Georgia. None of it compares to stock car racing.

In 1966 I returned to stock car racing and won $59,600 in prize money. Sixty per cent of that went to my car owner. However, endorsements and other considerations made it a great season. It's the money, plus the pride of winning, that makes the long hours and the hard work worthwhile. The hard work remains constant, but the prize money has been getting better every year. I won $69,585 in 1967, $118,492 in 1968 and $183,700 in 1969. I decided not to run for the championship in 1970 and entered only 19 races instead of the 51 I had been in during 1969. In spite of my greatly reduced schedule (I finished twenty-third in the point standings) my winnings for the year added up to $87,118.

I'm often asked if I'm afraid when I start a race. I don't think any race driver is afraid. If he were he certainly wouldn't get into the car in the first place. We all realize the danger involved and we are conscious of it. But we don't think about it. I'm no more afraid starting a race than I am starting down the ramp that leads into the 5 P.M. traffic on the Los Angeles Freeway.

I have butterflies—just like the baseball pitcher, the football quarterback or the boxer. That's excitement—not fear. Once they drop the green flag and it's every man for himself, you don't have time to think about anything but beating the man you've got to beat, and he's the one directly in front of you or directly behind you.

There have been some great drivers lost in the years I've been running the Grand National circuit. Fireball Roberts and Joe Weatherly are both gone, victims of freakish accidents. I learned a lot from both of them, and racing learned a lot from their tragic accidents.

Stock car racing is safer than ever. When I first ran on the high banks at Daytona, we struggled to reach the 160 mph mark. I won the Firecracker 250 there in 1961 by averaging 154 miles an hour. It was hairy at those speeds. But by 1970 we were running laps of over 190 mph, and the cars were a lot more stable because of added safety features and improved tires.

Stock car racing has come of age, and I'm happy to be a part of it. Perhaps we don't command the respect of the Indianapolis "500" drivers and the international stars of the road-racing set, but I feel the day is coming when the Daytona 500 will be bigger than the Indianapolis "500" and the stock car race driver will get national and international prestige comparable with that in other professional sports.

Then there will be more opportunities for the dozens of guys who are courageous and skilled but just haven't had the breaks that it takes to get the big headlines and make the big money.

As I said, stock car racing is two ends of the world, and there's a lot of work and heartache from the bottom to the top. There are nights of sleeping in the truck or working until daylight in the garage. There are nights of eating dust and wrecking equipment just to pick up a $15.00 tow fee. One race you're a hero and the next you're a bum.

But there's nothing like it—believe me. I'm proud to be a professional race driver, participating in the one sport that has never known a scandal. And I look to next year and the next as the National Association for Stock Car Racing continues to guide the relatively young sport to its place in the future. I see the $300,000 purses with a winner getting $100,000. I see bigger trophies and headlines. And I see the guy who struggled back in the pack with inferior equipment getting his share of the breaks and stepping up to collect his share of the rewards.

Stock car racing? A thing as small as a broken lug bolt can change everything in a matter of seconds. It's hard and it's dangerous, but there's something about seeing that checkered flag wave that makes it all worthwhile.

1

THE GRAND NATIONAL CIRCUIT

Brightly painted cars circle the track, the roar of unmuffled engines and the acrid smell of burning oil herald the start of a Grand National stock car race. Fans sitting in the first few rows brace themselves for an avalanche of noise and a cloud of dust mixed with burned rubber as the closely bunched cars approach the starter.

The green flag falls, and the steady roar of the engines rises to a crescendo as the cars charge across the start-finish line. The competition is furious, but the drivers who battle fender-to-fender and hub-to-hub don't take any chances With the machines hurtling around a narrow strip of asphalt at speeds ranging from 115 to 180 or more miles an hour on the superspeedways, there is room for only one mistake.

Advances in engineering have made race cars capable of withstanding the tremendous strain of high speeds, the rigors of long-distance events and even the occasional grinding crashes.

The "Granddaddy" of stock car sanctioning organizations is the National Association for Stock Car Auto Racing. The Grand National circuit is the top division of NASCAR and consists of the finest drivers, racing engineers, mechanics and pit crews who competed for more than $2.4 million in prize money during 1971. The season runs from January through December with approximately 35 races scheduled on tracks ranging from .5 of a mile to Talladega's 2.66-mile oval and Riverside's 2.62-mile road course. Auto racing's

The green flag falls and the steady roar of the engines rises to a crescendo as the cars charge across the start-finish line at the 1967 Daytona 500.

rise as a spectator sport has been meteoric, with more than 50 million paid attendance in 1971. Stock car events have attracted their share with more than 105,000 at the 1970 Daytona 500 and some 82,000 at the 1971 World 600 in Charlotte.

WHAT IS A GRAND NATIONAL RACE CAR?
Rules and Specifications

NASCAR Grand National races are open to American-made passenger car production sedans which are available to the general public. The cars must be steel-bodied models manufactured within two years prior to the current model. The cars are divided into two categories—standard and intermediate.

Category I cars are of standard size, such as Ford Galaxie, Dodge Polara, Plymouth Fury, etc. The category is limited to cars with a minimum wheelbase of 119 inches and a maximum engine size of 430-cubic-inch displacement. The cars must weigh at least 3,800 pounds including gas, water and oil ready to race. A maximum of one cubic inch is allowed for overboring due to cylinder wear.

The Category II cars fall in the intermediate range, such as Dodge Charger, Ford Torino, Chevrolet Monte Carlo, Pontiac GTO, Plymouth Road Runner, etc. This category is limited to cars with a minimum wheelbase of 115 inches, but less than 119 inches, and a maximum engine size of 430-cubic-inch displacement. One-cubic-inch overbore is allowed for cylinder wear. The Category II cars must weigh a minimum of 3,800 pounds ready to race.

NASCAR rules specify that the engine must be a regular production option of the manufacturer and that 500 bona fide units of the type of car and engine must have been sold to the public before the car or engine can be eligible for competition.

The NASCAR rules have set time limits for introduction of new models. Any car which has met the requirements by January 1 will be eligible to compete during that year.

New models or engines introduced between January 1 and April 15 will be eligible after April 15, provided the minimum of 500 units have been sold to the public. New models or engines introduced after April 15 will not be allowed to compete until the following year.

The original body dimensions must remain as they were when the car left the factory, with the exception of slight alterations for rear tire clearance. The frame and body cannot be lowered. The bodies must be complete and in good repair. The use of alloys or fiberglass replacement parts to save weight is forbidden. In the in-

The tire inspection window through which the driver may observe the wear of the tread on the right front tire.

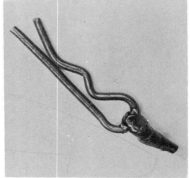

NASCAR safety rules demand that the hood and deck be securely fastened in place. A ¾" anchor post is welded to a reinforcing plate on each side of the car. The hood and deck are drilled out and a reinforcing collar plate (left) is applied to the sheet metal. The safety pin (right) is inserted to lock the hood or deck in place. The safety pins are attached to a steel cable and may be quickly removed or replaced.

---

terest of safety and handling, the rules were changed in 1967 to permit the use of a 1½-inch nonadjustable spoiler which may be attached to the rear deck lid.

The car floor must remain intact except for tire inspection windows, and the engine firewall must remain standard. No streamlining of the cars by using belly pans or an altered windshield angle is allowed. The headlights and taillights must be removed and the openings covered with sheet metal. Hood and trunk lids must have original type hinges and positive fasteners to insure they remain closed during competition.

Frames may be reinforced or altered to increase safety and to permit use of exhaust headers, additional shock absorbers and 9½-inch wheel rims. But the wheelbase must remain the same as manufactured in respect to measurements from front-door jam post to front axle.

Heavy duty springs may be used to beef up the suspension

system, providing they are similar to the original equipment. Sway bars may be reinforced and extra sway bars are permissible. Front-end suspension must be reinforced; the rules require heavy duty spindles and bearings. A maximum of four degrees of camber is allowed.

Both A-frames may be moved forward a maximum of one inch from the original position, but left and right must match. Wheel-base must conform to manufacturer's specifications plus or minus one and one-half inches. Front and rear tread must conform to manufacturer's specifications plus or minus one inch, with the variance allowed for reinforcing wheels.

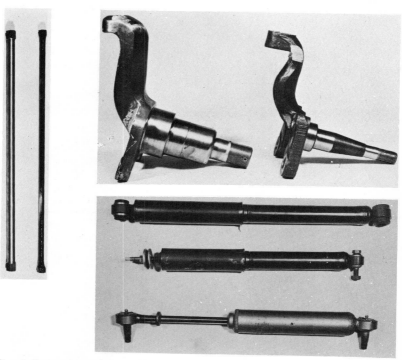

Specially made racing spindle (above left), made of heavy duty metal, is designed to take pounding never encountered by a passenger car. Spindle end is 1½″ thick compared to stock part's ¾″ (right). Torsion bar (outer left), also made of heavy duty material, is thicker to keep race car from leaning in turns and to level it out faster after hitting bumps. Racing bars range in thickness from 1³⁄₁₆″ to 1⁵⁄₁₆″. Stock part (left) is ⅞″. Stock Dodge shock absorbers (lower photo) are compared to the racing shock (bottom) which has thicker cylinder walls, valves, shaft, ends and mountings and comes in light, medium and heavy control combinations.

Minimum ground clearance of between 5 and 7½ inches must be maintained on the left side with a variance of no more than two inches higher on the right side. The oil pan and exhaust pipe must clear the ground by a minimum of four inches. The use of special devices to obtain minimum ground clearance is forbidden since these could become dislodged during competition. No mechanical or hydraulic device which will allow the driver to shift the weight distribution while the race car is in motion is permitted.

Mufflers must be removed, but the exhaust pipes used are optional as long as the inside diameter is no larger than four inches and meets NASCAR technical inspectors' approval.

Transmissions must be standard production and catalogued, and must be in full working order. Drive shaft and universals must be standard production only, and a special bracket must be installed on the drive shaft and mounted to the floor or a crossmember to prevent the drive shaft from dropping onto the race track during competition.

Full floating rear axles are compulsory, and limited slip differentials are legal. No quick-change rear ends are permitted. The rear axle ring and pinion may be of any ratio, but that usually is

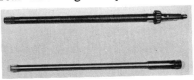

Standard axle (upper left) vs. racing axle, made of tougher metal to withstand conditions never encountered by a passenger car. Racing axles can be removed without dismantling wheel. A variety of differentials can be used depending upon the track. The 3.91 to 1 differential (left) would most likely be used at Darlington—a range anywhere from 2.85 to 1 to 2.95 to 1 would be used on Daytona's high banks. Photo (right) shows how shocks are mounted to lower control arm. Holes cut in front wheel wells connect shocks to specially designed shock mount frame.

governed by the length of the race track. NASCAR-approved differential oil coolers are allowed. Air lifts, coil-spring rubber inserts and additional shocks are permissible to improve handling. Interchangeable pitman arms may be used in the steering system along with reinforced tie rods, drag links and component parts.

Backing plates and brake drums may be drilled for better air circulation, and air scoops which meet NASCAR approval may be used. Any interchangeable brake and drum assembly may be used. Spot or disk brakes are limited to cars which offer them as standard factory equipment. Cars must be equipped with a complete set of bumpers. NASCAR recommends that bumpers be bolted to the fenders as a safety precaution and requires that the rear bumper be reinforced with channel iron.

Engine size is limited to 430 cubic inches, and the size of the engine must be painted on both sides of the hood in numerals at least 8 inches high. Internal porting, polishing and altering of motor parts are permitted. Oil coolers and oversize oil pans may be used if they are NASCAR approved.

Engines may be bored and stroked, providing the maximum displacement does not exceed the limits for the particular engine. The cylinder blocks must have standard external measurements, with the only permissible variation being the overbore.

The cylinder heads must be of standard production but internal alterations are permitted. The crankshaft must be of standard production design. The stroke may be increased or decreased, and balancing of the crank is allowed.

A ⅜-inch thick steel scattershield is required above the clutch and flywheel area. No changes from normal production are permitted in the bell housing. High-speed clutch assemblies are permitted, but NASCAR will not allow changes in the flywheel weight.

Rocker arm supports must be standard, and ball or roller-bearing rocker arms are not permitted unless they are standard equipment on volume production engines. Solid or hydraulic lifters are optional, but roller tappets are not permitted unless available on production engines. Any pistons are allowed as long as they are offered as optional equipment.

The ignition system must be standard for the car, and the automatic advance in the distributor must be in working condition. A transistorized system, approved by NASCAR, can be used along with any type points. Any brand of spark plugs may be used.

Batteries must remain under the hood and as near as possible to the original location. The generator or alternator system must be working and the self-starter must be in working condition. All cars must start under their own power. The only exception to this rule is pushing a car by hand in the pit area after the race is underway. A tow or push by another vehicle will result in disqualification.

Motor mounts must be reinforced and securely bolted. The engine cannot be moved forward or backward to achieve a more favorable weight distribution. Carburetors used on Grand National cars must be production models available from the manufacturer's line. No external alterations are allowed.

Rockerarm hemispherical head engines (Chrysler, Dodge and Plymouth) are restricted to one four-barrel carburetor with a maximum of $1\frac{11}{16}$-inch throttle bore (venturi area) when used with a box-type manifold. If a log-type manifold is used, one four-barrel with $1\frac{3}{4}$-inch throttle bore is allowed.

Overhead cam engines (Ford) are restricted to one four-barrel carburetor with $1\frac{11}{16}$-inch throttle bore.

Cars with approved-size engines (306 to 430 cubic inches) may be required to use a carburetor restrictor plate furnished by NASCAR. The size of the plates was changed several times in 1971 and the plates were finally eliminated in September. NASCAR substituted the use of varying size carburetor sleeves.

The intake manifold must be of conventional design and readily available to participants, but there are no limitations on the materials used in the manifold. Carburetor jets may be of any size. Wedges to level the carburetor to compensate for constant lean to the left are permitted. Heat risers may be blocked off, and any NASCAR-approved gasoline filter may be employed. Fuel injection systems or superchargers are not allowed.

Cars will be fueled only with gasoline, and NASCAR reserves the right to insist that all competitors use the same type of gasoline. Fuel cells (spongy rubber cells developed by Firestone as a protection against fire) are required on all cars. The first fuel cells were installed in 1966 and were credited with saving several lives in serious wrecks involving the rear end of the car.

NASCAR requires that the fuel cell be encased in a 20-gauge steel container (9 x 17 x 33 inches) divided into two sections as nearly equal as possible. The fuel-cell container may be fastened to the trunk floor or recessed but must be located as far forward in the trunk as possible. There must be two steel straps, running lengthwise and across, to hold the container in place. A one-inch vent to the outside of the body must exit near the left rear light. The filler neck may not exceed $2\frac{1}{4}$ inches in outside diameter.

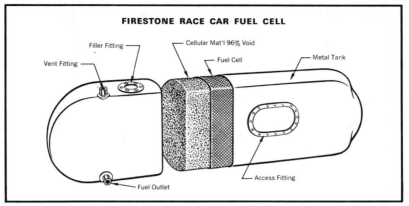

Fuel cells are required on all cars. The Firestone fuel cells come in various shapes and sizes.

The maximum fuel-cell capacity, including filler spout, is 22 gallons, and the cell must have a removable drain plug, or the owner faces the prospect of having the tank removed for inspection. A special firewall of 20-gauge steel must be installed between the trunk and the interior of the car for the protection of the driver.

Electric fuel pumps are forbidden and water cooling of the fuel pump is illegal. Fuel lines may be relocated between the fuel tank and the fuel pump to prevent vapor lock. Neoprene hose not to exceed ½-inch inside diameter may be used in place of the standard hose. No electric motors are permitted in the trunk, and no icing or cooling of fuel is permitted anywhere in the racing area.

Wheels must be reinforced and all four must be the same

A front-view comparison of wheels, the standard 14-inch wheel at the left and the reinforced 15-inch racing wheel on the right. Notice the extra heavy welds and larger lug bolt openings.

size and diameter. Either 14- or 15-inch diameter wheels are permitted but all four must be the same in size. Maximum wheel rim width allowed is 9½ inches.

NASCAR requires all four tires to be of the same size, tread design and make. The same type tread and grade of rubber must be available to all competitors. Cross-grooving of treads or use of knobbies, drag tires or power-grip baldies is not permitted. Recaps are not permitted on any track over a mile in length. Even on the shorter tracks, paved or dirt, a competitor must use NASCAR-approved recaps which are limited to ten inches in width. Special racing rubber with standard treads is permissible. Safety tires with inner liners are compulsory on all NASCAR superspeedways and other tracks as specified by NASCAR.

Safety Requirements

A steel roll-bar cage is compulsory in all Grand National cars and must meet NASCAR approval. The cage must be joined at the top and sides. Side roll bars are required, and they must extend through the doors, with a minimum of two bars on the right and four on the left. The roll bars set in the driver's door must have some outward arch for added protection. The roll bars must be of at least 1¾ inches outside diameter and welded in place. Walls of the pipe *must* be at least .090 inches thick.

Buck and Buddy Baker look over the four protecting roll bars on the driver's side of the car.

Standard seats and cushions must be removed; factory-made bucket seats are mandatory. NASCAR does not permit homemade or aluminum seats. Tracks on adjustable seats must be bolted or welded solidly to the roll-bar frame and floor to prevent shifting in an accident. Extra padding on the right side of the seat is required. The center post of the steering wheel also must be padded with at least two inches of foam rubber or other protective material.

There must be a full windshield and rear window in each car. The rear window must be permanently closed with two 1- x ⅛-inch steel straps. Side windows must conform to standard thickness and size, and equipment to raise or lower them must remain as original. The rear-view mirror must not extend outside the car.

NASCAR requires seat belts and shoulder harness as well as a safety helmet. Seat belts must be three inches wide and have a quick release. The shoulder belt must come down over the shoulder to prevent more than a specified amount of forward travel. NASCAR also recommends a head rest bolted to the roll-bar cage to avoid whiplash injuries.

Each car is required to carry an approved foam-type fire extinguisher securely mounted within easy reach of the driver, and the pit crew must have an approved extinguisher at hand. Since 1964 most drivers have carried special extinguishers which will completely fill the interior of a race car with foam in less than two seconds.

How to Build a Grand National Race Car
An Interview with Cotton Owens

Everett "Cotton" Owens is a pioneer in the stock car racing field. He has grown with the sport that has changed from a small town thrill show to a sport of international prominence.

The forty-nine-year-old Spartanburg, South Carolina, garage owner began his career on NASCAR's Modified Circuit in 1946. Driving cars tooled in his own garage, Owens became known as "King of the Modifieds," winning the U.S. Modified title three times and the rugged Modified-Sportsman feature on the old beach and road course at Daytona Beach twice.

Campaigning in a souped-up Dodge in 1950, he won 54 feature races throughout the South, including 24 in succession.

The 5-foot, 4-inch 145-pound mechanical wizard has been just as successful in Late Model stock car racing. He won the 1957 Speedweeks feature at Daytona Beach. That same year he qualified for the pole position in the Southern 500 and finished second.

Owens drove to a world record (143 mph) in qualifying for the first Daytona 500 on the new Daytona International Speedway in 1959. Then, in 1960, he averaged 149.6 mph to set a new qualifying record for the Southern 500 at Darlington, South Carolina. He was second in the Atlanta 500 in 1961, and owned and built the Pontiac Bobby Johns drove to victory in the same race. Since 1963 Owens has been operating a stable of Dodges on the NASCAR circuit under the sponsorship of Carolina Dodge Dealers Association.

With the growth of interest in stock car racing have come a million and one questions. One of the most important of these is: "Who wins races—the driver or the mechanic?"

"It's a hard question to answer," says Cotton Owens. "Drivers get the glory and most of the pay check, deservedly, too. After all—they take the major risks. But real satisfaction goes to the mechanic. Having spent more than twenty years as both mechanic and driver, I feel qualified to say that most races are won in the garages."

SAFETY FIRST "Before a driver can get the checkered flag he must have a car that is not only fast, but stout and, most important, safe," Owens says. "With that in mind I try to stress safety and strength in setting up race cars. When I feel that I have covered every possible cause of trouble, then I begin concentrating on making the car fast.

"It would be quite simple to build a superfast car without regard to safety. In some types of competition, fiberglass bodies, aluminum bumpers and firewalls and cast-aluminum roll bars are allowed. Thankfully, we have rules to protect us from ourselves.

"In NASCAR we have stringent rules with inspections at every track. NASCAR is, I guess, the largest auto racing organization in the world, with more than fifteen thousand active members. Bill Gazaway, chief technical inspector for NASCAR, is one of the fairest men I know."

TOUGH INSPECTIONS "In building several Dodge race cars, I keep testing myself on each phase of the work. 'Will the inspectors okay this?' If the answer is yes, then I know I'm doing a good and safe job. With the exception of a few engine refinements, the only changes that are allowed are those which make the cars safe to drive. It is

26

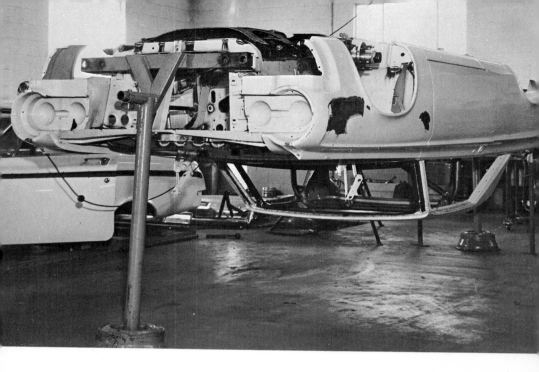

A "bottom's up" automobile is never a nice sight to a race driver, but in this position it is being constructed at Cotton Owens' Garage in Spartanburg, South Carolina. The car is turned this way to give welders easy access to all parts as it is made ready for the Grand National Circuit.

NASCAR's adamant stand on safety which makes it the safest racing circuit."

All ornaments and extras which could vibrate loose must be removed. All parts which will be subjected to more strain than normal highway driving must be reinforced or replaced with heavier, stronger equipment.

"I always try to strip the car of all excess weight and then put back only what is necessary to make it safe. NASCAR rules decree it must weigh 9.36 pounds per cubic inch of engine displacement. A Dodge we just completed tipped the scales at 3,992 pounds with a 426 engine. If we run a 405-cubic-inch engine we can remove weight to meet the lower specifications."

EXTRA WEIGHT REMOVED "We start building by tearing down," Owens explains. Here's what's done:

The car is completely dismantled inside and out. All weather stripping is removed. Undercoating is chipped off. Floor mats, seats, upholstery, spare tire, wiring, window garnish moldings and door handles, chrome ornament and dash instruments are cast aside. Then Owens starts to build a race car.

Because of the high speeds these cars travel (up to 180-plus mph), special valved shock absorbers are used to prevent the car from being bouncy and becoming airborne.

CHASSIS "BEEFED UP" Because race cars are subjected to terrific stress, the stock product is beefed up wherever possible. All chassis joints are rewelded. The front frame rails are plated with one-eighth-inch steel and completely rewelded. Fishplates are added on the rear frame. A roll-bar cage is attached both to the structural sills on the body and to the frame rails. This stiffens the entire chassis, but is designed primarily to protect the driver.

HEAVIER STEERING COMPONENTS Upper and lower control arms are reinforced. The K-frame is completely rewelded. Standard tie rods are replaced with heavy duty truck steering connections. Because of extra heavy torsion bars, two shock absorbers are installed on each front wheel. A heavy duty sway bar supplements the shock system and keeps the front of the car steady at high speeds.

A special forged steel spindle is installed along with a heavy duty steel hub which carries much larger bearings. The front suspension is the stock item slightly modified. Standard woven brake linings are replaced with heat-treated Cerametalix linings. Whereas the woven linings tend to harden and fade in extreme heat, the Cerametalix linings will improve.

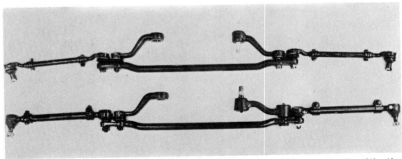

This is a comparison of the standard steering linkage (top) with the heavy duty racing linkage (bottom), which is heavier throughout. The idler arm is inverted in order to lower linkage.

REAR SUSPENSION MOST VITAL   The rear suspension, Owens says, is the heart of the race car since it controls weight balance and therefore handling on the race track. Balance is an objective. However, rear suspension must be set to transfer weight to the left side to offset the natural shift to the right when making that hard left turn on the tracks. To accomplish this, all spring shackles and hangers are removed, and adjustment brackets installed. The brackets have holes drilled at various levels to transfer the weight to the left side, depending on the bank of the track.

REAR SPRINGS ADJUSTABLE   On the Dodge race cars Owens uses the standard spring (five leaves) on the left side. The right spring is de-arced, and two extra leaves plus a torque leaf are added.

"We attain better results by using stock parts wherever necessary and modifying them to our own situation," Owens says. "This is especially true in setting up the Dodge because ruggedness is already built into most parts."

The two rear shock absorbers are replaced with four extra-long, heavy duty shocks. Shock brackets are extended into the trunk of the car. A special shock bracket, extending below the axle hous-

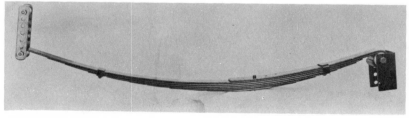

The rear springs are bolstered by the addition of extra leaves. Some mechanics use heavy truck springs, but Owens prefers lighter springs which permit flexibility in the rear suspension for better handling characteristics. The heavy duty front and rear spring hangers are adjustable so that the car can be "set" at just the right angle for each track.

ing, is necessary to take care of the extra length. Adjustment holes are drilled. During extremely hot weather racing, a differential cooling system is added which enables grease to be pumped through a radiator located in the trunk.

DOZEN GEARS USED Owens and his crew carry a dozen or more differentials in equipment stock because of extreme differences in tracks encountered during the fifty-odd NASCAR races each season.

"Our goal is to get our horsepower output at 5600 to 5800 rpm," Owens says. "We feel we can keep the engine operating for distance races in that range. Then we must use a gear which will get us the necessary power and speed to be a front runner."

The 18 gear ratios used in Dodge racing cars range from 2.76 to 6.17. The differential shown (left) is the 3.55 which is considered best for the 1½-mile ovals at Charlotte and Atlanta.

SAFETY HUBS Because a safety hub is not only essential, but required by NASCAR, the width of the axle housing must be cut down. The stock housing is put in a lathe and the ends cut off. New machined ends are pressed in and welded, ready to receive the full-floating axle assembly.

"The full-floater, which I consider one of the best developments for safety and performance in racing in recent years, can be assembled in several ways. All get the same results," Owens says.

The axle shaft is virtually "floating" on tapered bearings and does not support the weight of the car. This weight is transferred to the axle housing. A special adapter is pressed into the housing. Then a large bearing hub is secured to the adapter. The stud hub, carrying extra heavy duty lug bolts, is attached next.

This view of the full-floating rear hub shows how the brake drum is secured by the stud hub before the free-floating axle is inserted and locked on.

FLANGED AXLES   The axle hub flange is inserted over the lug bolts. The wheel, cut out and drilled to fit over this big assembly, is attached to the stud hub instead of the axle, as in nonfloating rear ends.

"The weight of the car is actually transferred to the housing through the stud hub," Owens explains. "Should an axle break, the old 'lock-up' problem will not occur, and the car will continue rolling."

The wheels (15 x 9½ inches) are special also, two inches wider and reinforced. Special rubber compounds are used in the production of the wider-tread racing tires. Both Goodyear and Firestone offer a wide variety.

BODY WEIGHT REDUCED   "Now that we have covered the suspension and wheels, let's take a closer look at the body," Owens continues. "We have added weight through the use of bigger parts and additional plating and welds. Now, we must take off weight, and the best place to do it is on the body. Floor mats, headlining and extra seats are removed. Instruments and gauges that we don't use are removed."

NASCAR requires that full windshield and rear window be in good condition. All side-window glass must conform to original size and thickness, and all opening and closing equipment must remain. However, drivers are allowed to race with windows down and/or removed on smaller tracks, and most do.

STRESS SAFETY FOR DRIVER   Interior installations include the roll-bar cage and a bucket seat, angled toward the left side and padded on the right side to hold the driver firmly in place. A steel firewall replaces the rear seat to lessen danger from gasoline tank explosion. A hand fire extinguisher (powder type) is mounted near the driver's right hand. A water thermos is attached behind the driver. The driver sucks the water from a tube. Roll bars must be constructed of steel tubing, not less than 1¾ inches in outside diameter with walls not less than .090 inches thick.

SAFETY HARNESS A heavy duty safety belt with an aviation-type shoulder harness (another NASCAR requirement) is installed. The steering wheel hub is also heavily padded. The stock instrument cluster is replaced with a tachometer. A water temperature gauge showing up to 250 degrees is installed. An oil pressure gauge showing 0 to 100 pounds and a 100- to 325-degree oil temperature gauge are installed. A 0- to 10-pound gauge showing fuel pressure at the point of entrance to carburetor is also a necessity.

DOORS BOLTED SHUT The glove compartment is sealed and doors are locked shut from the inside with special brackets and bolts. Wide strips of asbestos tape cover window frames when the glass is not rolled up. This prevents shattered glass from spewing into the car in the event the door is sideswiped.

Interior installations include the heavy duty roll-bar cage and a bucket seat which is angled toward the left side and padded on the right side to hold the driver firmly in place.

This interior view shows the heavily padded steering wheel and the altered instrument cluster which contains a tachometer, a water temperature gauge, an oil pressure gauge, an oil temperature gauge and a fuel pressure gauge.

CHROME TAPE USED The exterior body is only slightly altered. Headlights are removed and the openings covered with aluminum. All chrome and ornaments are removed and replaced with chrome tape. Positive fasteners are installed on the hood and trunk lid. Holes drilled into the hood and deck lid in line with pins fastened to the body are reinforced, top and bottom, with steel collar shields. Large safety clips, attached to the body with steel cable, fit through the pin eyes and secure the hood and deck lid.

BAFFLE FUEL TANK NASCAR rules limit fuel tanks to 22 gallons capacity. However, they can be modified for both safety and practical racing conditions. The stock 22-gallon tank has a fuel cell that prevents the tank from bursting open in case of accident. During competition, centrifugal force pushes the fuel to the outside of the tank. The fuel pickup line is relocated on the right side. The breather vent is enlarged to one inch and moved from the spout to the top of the tank. A rubber hose is attached there, inside the trunk, and extends out to a spot higher than the filler neck. The filler neck must be stock in diameter (2¼ inches) but may be lengthened to facilitate fast fueling. A conventional cap is used. It is attached to the car with a cable to prevent it from being dropped or from falling off during the race.

K-FRAME REINFORCED While the engine compartment must remain stock, there are some changes necessary—always for safety. The K-frame is removed and completely rewelded. The motor mounts are also reinforced by approved NASCAR methods. There are two cooling systems, one for the engine itself and one for oil. The latter

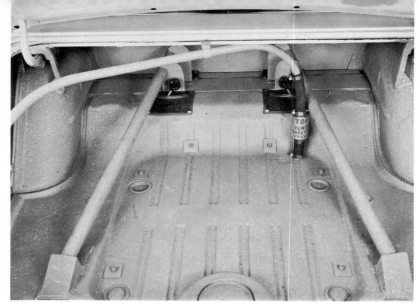

This view of the trunk of one of Cotton Owens' racers shows a lot of safety. Steel bars bracing the roll-bar cage inside the car extend through the trunk and are secured to the body. Extra-stiff shocks, made longer to allow more travel, are attached to the roll bar braces. The safety valve at right prevents gasoline from spilling from the fuel tank in the event the car overturns.

This view of the left side front suspension was photographed from near the door on the driver's side. Heavy duty linkage leading to the steering gear box emphasizes strength. Torsion bar is standard, smaller than bar on right side (not shown) where punishment is focused during race on oval tracks. Heavy duty shocks stand more upright on left side. Reinforced K-frame can be seen in background.

is an added option brought about by the high speeds the stock cars attain on the larger NASCAR tracks.

BIG RADIATOR   The radiator core has a greater capacity than the factory version and is reinforced to guard against vibration and designed to combat dirt clogging. Circular fan guards are added. The oil cooler, a miniature radiator, is also located in the grille section.

"The engine is stock," Owens emphasizes. "NASCAR officials conduct a thorough technical inspection before each race and then seal the engine. Lift a hood in the garage or pit areas and you have at least one technical official looking over your shoulder. When they say stock—they mean stock."

The engine is the single four-barrel, 426 Dodge Hemi-Charger. It is designed for supervised competition both on the speedways and drag strips. It is rated at 425 horsepower, but when blueprinted, "a Cotton Owens Hemi-Charger engine pulls 550 horsepower," he says.

SINGLE FOUR-BARREL CARB   "NASCAR's rules limit us to the use of just one four-barrel carburetor," Owens explains. "Without giving away any secrets to my competition, I can say briefly that this loss of horsepower is offset by NASCAR's approval of the use of high performance camshafts. By tearing the engine down and balancing all parts perfectly, we are able to solve some problems before they occur. We measure the combustion and valve chambers to make sure they are exactly equal."

HEAVY DUTY VALVE GEAR   The standard Hemi-Charger engine has high strength, forged aluminum pistons with 11 to 1 compression ratio. Cylinder heads have larger ports, streamlined intake valves and larger exhaust valves. No polishing is allowed. The high lift camshaft is designed for speeds in excess of 6000 rpm. The valve gear has dual high load springs and heavy duty retainers. The ignition system has a special distributor cam and dual breaker points.

"Because of heat problems we are allowed to enlarge our oil pan. The stock pan has a five-quart capacity," says Owens. "We enlarge ours to hold eight quarts in the pan itself and a total capacity of ten for pan and engine, going two over to allow for the cooler. This larger oil pan is also baffled to keep the oil from being forced to the right side."

USE STOCK HEADERS   High capacity, cast, streamlined exhaust headers are fitted to straight exhaust pipes—not more than four inches inside diameter. The powerful Hemi-Charger engine is linked to the running gear with a standard, four-speed, synchromesh transmission. There is a heavy duty Hurst floor shift.

"They say a race car is never complete, and I agree," Owens says. "When you've finished building your car and think you have it ready for the track, close inspection will always turn up ways and means to make it safer, more durable and faster."

PROTECT GAS TANK "A piece of metal can puncture a fuel tank and put you out of a race. In addition to covering the bottom of the tank with a heavy asbestos padding, we box it in with a metal shield and attach it tight to the body with four metal straps. Protective shields must also be added to the oil pan, flywheel housing and, when it is used, the differential cooler."

PIT CREW TRAINING "Maintaining a race car requires not only a lot of old elbow grease, but a modern garage with modern equipment. A good pit crew is vital to success. We have a great crew. Tire change, gas fill and a clean windshield have to be done in less than twenty-five seconds.

"I have found it costs about $20,000 to build a good stock race car, including the cost of the car. It costs a lot more to make a consistent winner. But the cleaner and safer the equipment—the better your chances. At least those are the odds I try to carry with me to the race tracks."

Research and Development

For the past decade every race track in the country, especially where stock cars compete, has become a proving ground for manufacturers or accessories. Auto racing has contributed greatly to advancements made in the production cars which Aunt Minnie drives to the supermarket and to which Uncle Joe hitches his boat for the weekend fishing trip.

Better and safer tires head a long list of technical advances which are pretty much taken for granted. Included on the list are high-compression engines, better burning fuel, rear-view mirrors, seat belts, four-wheel brakes, dual braking systems, more efficient ignition systems, better ride characteristics through shock absorbers and sway bars and the development of better, longer lasting engine metals. All these contributions have made the car which comes off the showroom floor safer to drive and have given it better handling characteristics.

The development of longer lasting lubricants has changed

the lube schedule from every 1,000 miles to 6,000 miles. The day is coming when it won't be necessary to lubricate the car at all, except to change the oil. During the early days of racing only one or two of the oil companies showed any interest. Today a half-dozen oil companies have extensive racing programs.

Accessory firms, including tire companies, brake manufacturers, spark plug makers and countless others, are spending more money on racing than the auto manufacturers.

Most top Grand National drivers agree that tire development has been one of the most significant changes over the years. In 1950 more than 90 cars entered the Southern 500 at Darlington with regular tires. Johnny Mantz tried a special set of tires prepared by Firestone. As a result he was the only driver who didn't have tire problems. Mantz made two stops for tires while the second- and third-place cars used a total of 70 tires.

Firestone and Goodyear have been providing tires for Grand National race cars for more than 20 years. Firestone withdrew from Grand National competition after 1969, but still provides tires for Sportsman and Modified competition as well as for other forms of racing. The size of tires created especially for racing has increased

Bill McCrary, manager of Firestone's racing division, illustrates the difference between a passenger car tire (left) and a stock car tire designed in 1964 for Darlington International Raceway. Tires have grown wider and wider each year as can be seen by the 1967 stock car tire, which Gene White, Firestone race tire distributor, is inspecting.

Highly skilled Firestone tire engineers take tire temperatures after each run during practice and qualifying and also keep a close check on track temperatures and conditions. These are extremely important for both the driver and his mechanic.

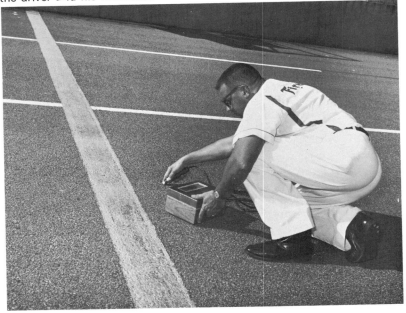

along with stock car competition. Normal passenger tires place a little over five inches of rubber on the ground while racing tires are almost a foot wide. NASCAR specifications limit tire width to $11^{11}\!/_{16}$ inches. These tires place a footprint of at least 10 inches on the track surface.

The development of the safety inner-liner in 1965 eliminated many of those jolting trips to the guard rail as a tire popped. The extra cushion of air in the inner-liner gives the driver precious seconds to regain control of a ton and a half of racing metal before it is too late.

Each major tire company has 25 men working full time on racing endeavors. The goal is to produce a tire which will last the entire 500 miles without danger to the driver. In most 500-mile races, outside tires are changed at every gas stop because the two tires can be changed in less time than the car requires to take on a full load of gas. Although the tires may have many miles of wear left, the change, in most instances, is a precaution since tires are much cheaper to replace than a bent race car.

Safer tires, better burning fuels, more efficient lubricants, longer lasting engine metals—all these and more—make for better racing and more reliable production cars.

PERSONALITIES

Off the track the Grand National drivers are just about as diverse a group of men as can be found. They come from all walks of life and have varied educational backgrounds. On the race track it's another story. Each driver shares in the other's preparation—in spirit at least. In many instances he helps out by loaning spare parts, sharing pit crews or just feeling a little heartache for a friend who has had bad luck.

David Pearson

David Pearson has earned two of the most coveted titles in NASCAR since breaking into the big time in 1960 as NASCAR Rookie of the Year.

The Spartanburg, South Carolina, driver piloted a Ray Fox Pontiac to three superspeedway wins during his second year. In the intervening five years, Pearson was unable to win in a race of 250 miles or longer. With 15 victories in short track events in 1966 Dave captured the 1966 NASCAR Grand National Point Championship.

Pearson went on to capture the 1968 and 1969 GN point championships, driving the Holman-Moody Ford. He is the second

David Pearson

Fred Lorenzen

driver to win that title three times. Pearson has won more than 60 GN events and earned more than $700,000 in prize money.

Fred Lorenzen

Fred Lorenzen, a carpenter from Elmhurst, Illinois, who retired from racing in 1967, had captured the affection of thousands of race fans wherever he appeared.

When the former Modified pilot came South in 1960 as a protege of Ralph Moody, he was described as a driver "who couldn't find his way around a cornfield in a tractor." That was before Moody's coaching began to sink in.

During his first season with the famed racing team of Holman and Moody, neither Moody nor Lorenzen were satisfied, but Moody recognized the spark or whatever it is that makes a great driver. At the time of his retirement Lorenzen was the all-time big money winner in NASCAR Grand National circles. Fred spent as much time under his car as he did behind the wheel in an effort to learn more about what he could do to improve his performance on the track.

Lorenzen returned to racing in 1970 in a Dodge and raced an STP-sponsored Plymouth for Nichels Engineering in 1971. Many felt that the "Golden Boy" had lost his touch during his three-year layoff, but Fred quickly showed that he could be one of the world's best stock car drivers when he had competitive equipment. Lorenzen was hurt in a spectacular accident during practice at Darlington in 1971, but was back racing the following month.

Buck and Buddy Baker

Buck Baker of Charlotte, North Carolina, has started to pick and choose his races after a career which has spanned a quarter of a century of racing and has given him a son who may exceed his father's greatest accomplishments. The fifty-three-year-old driver owns three wins at the famed Southern 500 at Darlington.

One of the early drivers on the NASCAR circuit, Buck drove the famous hemi-powered Chryslers back in 1955 and 1956. Always quick to jump into anything with four wheels and an engine, Buck could be found racing Modifieds at a dirt track in Greenville, South Carolina, one night and the next day running a 600-mile race back in Charlotte with little or no sleep. A close friend of Little Joe Weatherly, who died in a crash at Riverside, California, in 1964, Buck is a member of the seat-of-the-pants fraternity of drivers who would rather race than eat. Buck races strictly on the Grand American

41

circuit now and was involved in the point championship race during 1970 and 1971.

His strapping six-foot, five-inch son, Buddy, raced with his father's team until 1966 when a spot became available in Ray Fox's Dodge. Buddy moved from Ray Fox to the Cotton Owens Dodge team where he stayed until the major factory cutback at the end of 1970 when he was chosen to drive a 1971 Dodge prepared by Petty Engineering. The younger Baker's career, slow getting started, has zoomed toward the same stardom enjoyed by his father.

Fireball Roberts

Perhaps no one driver ever captured the imagination of racing fans across the Southeast as did the late Fireball Roberts. The Daytona Beach driver made the cars bearing No. 22 famous as he stuck his foot through the firewall and into the carburetor at every race track where he competed.

The Fireball got his nickname as a baseball pitcher, but the name fit just as well on the race track. Fireball set qualifying records at every track he visited and won a number of superspeedway victories before his death in a fiery crash at the Charlotte Motor Speedway during the 1964 World 600.

Bobby Isaac

Robert Vance Isaac, better known as Bobby, teamed with K&K Insurance in a three-year effort to capture the 1970 GN Point Championship.

The Catawba, North Carolina, native was virtually unknown in Grand National competition until 1968. Isaac's name was a household word around small dirt tracks in North and South Carolina and he had some GN experience, but with very little success, winning only one race.

Isaac has captured more than 35 Grand National events and earned about $400,000 in prize money. The former mill hand holds the world's record for a closed course set November 25, 1970 at Talladega Raceway with a speed of 201.104 miles an hour. He went to the Salt Flats in Utah in September of 1971 to set 28 world speed records for a stock car.

Bobby and Donnie Allison

The Allison brothers of Hueytown, Alabama, are one of the most potent brother racing combinations ever to appear in Grand National competition.

Although the brothers race for different teams, Bobby and

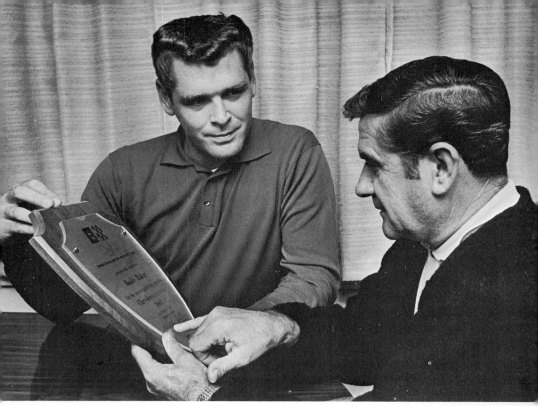

Buck and Buddy Baker

Fireball Roberts

Bobby Isaac

Donnie have won more than 30 Grand National events and carried off more than $750,000 in prize money. Both are well known on the Late Model Sportsman and Modified tracks throughout the south and Bobby lays claim to two national titles in the Late Model Sportsman Division (1962 and 1963).

Donnie has driven for Banjo Matthews and the Wood Brothers and is a regular at Indianapolis in an A. J. Foyt car. Bobby has driven for Mario Rossi and now wheels the Holman-Moody Ford entry.

Charlie Glotzbach

Chargin' Charlie Glotzbach got his big break when Paul Goldsmith decided to hang up his helmet. The Edwardsville, Indiana, driver ran a few races in 1960 and 1961, but didn't really make an impression until he got the Nichels Engineering ride under the tutelage of Goldsmith.

The shy trucking company owner drives with his foot in the carburetor and got the nod from Junior Johnson when he decided to build a Chevrolet in 1971 for Grand National competition.

Glotzbach and Johnson quickly showed that the team could produce a competitive car and they proved to be a major drawing card during the 1971 season. Mechanical failures sidelined the car several times, but Glotzbach and the Chevrolet always ran up front as long as the car would run.

Lee and Richard Petty

Another famous father-son team which has etched its name across NASCAR record pages is that of Poppa Lee and son Richard Petty of Randleman, North Carolina. A thundering crash at Daytona in 1961 ended Poppa Lee's career as a driver after three GN Point Championships and a total of fifty-four wins, but it opened the door for a racing team consisting of the entire family. Richard's brother Maurice does the engine work, Poppa Lee is the mastermind and chassis man and Richard drives.

Virtually every time Richard Petty enters a race, he adds a new record to the books. Richard is the first GN driver to win more than $1 million in prize money (more than $1,075,000 by 1971 season); he also has won more races (136 through 1971) and more money in a single season (more than $250,000 in 1971).

Petty owns the most superspeedway wins (13). He has won at every major track in the south except Charlotte, and has won the most races in one season (27 in 1967) and the most consecutive wins (10 in 1967). Richard has competed in 560 Grand National races,

Lee and Richard Petty

Bill Dennis

Joe Frasson

won 136, finished in the top five 328 times and finished in the top ten 395 times.

The affable driver shows no signs of slowing down at the ripe old age of 36, although he has been involved in several major accidents including a hair-raiser at Darlington in the 1970 Rebel 400. Richard's car struck the fourth turn wall, careered into the pit road retaining wall and rolled end-over-end and then sideways all the way to the start/finish line. Richard escaped with a dislocated shoulder.

Rookies

New drivers appear each year, either graduating from the Sportsman and Modified ranks or trying their luck in the stockers. Bill Dennis of Richmond, Virginia, beat out Joe Frasson of Golden Valley, Minnesota, and Jim Vandiver of Charlotte, North Carolina, for the honor of Rookie of the Year in 1970.

Dennis campaigned in 25 races and finished in the top 10 on five occasions. Dennis earned $15,630 in his first full season in a Chevelle and Mercury.

In 1971 Walter Ballard of Houston, Texas, was selected Rookie of the Year over a large crop of other contenders, including Maynard Troyer of Spencerport, New York; Richard Brown of Claremont, North Carolina; Dean Dalton of Asheville, North Carolina; Charlie Roberts of Anniston, Alabama, and Marv Acton of Porterville, California. Ballard, who sold his garage business to become a full-time racer, was presented with a new passenger car by the Air Lift Company of Lansing, Michigan.

Walter campaigned in 36 events and recorded three finishes in the top five and 11 in the top 10 and won $22,608.

Independents

Racing gets in the blood, whether you are a spectator, driver or mechanic. It has been said that racers have oil instead of blood in their veins, and the independent drivers come closest to fitting this description.

Wendell Scott of Danville, Virginia, came up through the Modified ranks competing in South Boston, Danville, Richmond and Martinsville, all in Virginia. Wendell faced double-barreled problems since he is a Negro. As a matter of fact, he is the only black driver on the Grand National circuit. Wherever there is a race, Wendell is there.

A first-class pilot, Wendell has always had to compete with secondhand equipment. In 1966 he bought the car Fred Lorenzen

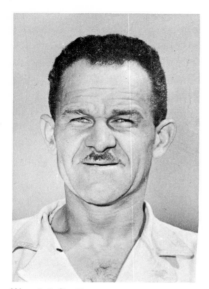

Wendell Scott

James Hylton

Elmo Langley

flipped six times at Riverside, fixed it up and drove it in more than 40 races during the year.

James Hylton of Inman, South Carolina, broke into racing as a driver in 1966 after an internship as mechanic for Ned Jarrett and Dick Hutcherson. Since then Hylton, a true independent, has finished second three times in the GN point race, third twice and seventh once.

Hylton has won only one Grand National race (Richmond, Virginia) but in 269 events he has finished in the top ten 208 times.

Elmo Langley held down a regular job in Landover, Maryland, and raced the GN circuit whenever he could. In 1966 he moved to Charlotte, North Carolina, and went racing full time entering 47 of 49 races, taking home more than $19,000 in prize money and finishing 11th in the point standings. Since then Elmo has finished in the top ten places in the point standings every year and in 1971 he won $57,037.

Car Owners and Builders

While drivers receive most of the acclaim around a race track, there are certain car builders who have a reputation which gives them equal billing. Some are former drivers. Others are "racing engineers," who crave speed and the satisfaction of being able to build the better race car. A half dozen or so of these men have shown over the years that they can and do build the fastest cars.

Ray Fox stood beside Buddy Baker in the garage area at Charlotte Motor Speedway as a photographer posed the pair. "Look up, Ray. We want to be sure everyone gets to see Buddy's mechanic's face," the photographer ordered.

The tall Daytona Beach racing magician simply turned his back and wouldn't pose until the photographer changed "mechanic" to "car builder." The intense pride of those who make the drivers' glory possible shows only rarely but it is there. The friendly rivalry between wrench turners is subdued but intense.

John Holman and Ralph Moody formed a racing team in 1957. Ralph is a former driver, who many think was one of the all-time greats. At one time during his career, Ralph had won so many races in Norfolk, Virginia, that the track promoter barred the gate when he appeared and then refused to sell him a ticket so he could watch the race.

With Holman providing the engineering brains and Moody the practical know-how, the name Holman-Moody has become internationally famous in racing circles. Stock cars, Ford's road-racing equipment and marine racing engines come from the three branches

Ray Fox

John Holman and Ralph Moody

Smokey Yunick

Ray Nichels

of Holman-Moody. Much of Ford's racing success can be attributed to this well-known team.

Ray Nichels of Highland, Indiana, has been working on race cars since he was fifteen. A wall clock in the Nichels garage bears the inscription, "Ray Nichels, M.D." Everyone says the initials stand for "Doctor of Motors." Anyone who has ever raced against Nichels' cars can testify about how many times he has effected a "cure."

Nichels had such top-notch drivers as Paul Goldsmith in NASCAR and Don White in USAC. The drivers come to him. Every independent or would-be race car driver would give more than he would like to admit to pilot one of Nichels' cars.

That cowboy hat seen at the tracks belongs to Smokey Yunick and "The Best Damn Garage in Town." Yunick's hat has become just as much a part of the racing scene as the superswift cars he builds.

His black and gold cars with No. 22, driven by Fireball Roberts, were sure to be out front in qualifying. Recently the number and driver have changed, but the equipment is still on a par with anything on the race track.

Cotton Owens earned his nickname from his extremely light blond hair which makes him easy to spot in the pits. After years as a driver, Cotton turned to building cars in order to stay near the sport which had gotten into his blood. The efforts brought success everywhere but on the superspeedways for the team of Owens and his former driver, David Pearson.

Banjo Matthews of Asheville, North Carolina, hung up his helmet and tried to settle down, but the thunder of racing kept echoing through the North Carolina mountains, and he answered the call as a car builder. Bobby Johns took a turn behind the wheel of one of his cars. Cale Yarborough also pushed a Banjo car as hard as it would go and did well. In 1967 Banjo built the car which A. J. Foyt piloted in FIA-sanctioned NASCAR events.

Glen and Leonard Wood live in a small town in Virginia, and the Wood Brothers' racing team is perhaps its biggest claim to fame. Stuart is in the heart of the Carolinas and Virginia Modified territory. Their reputation for speedy servicing is such that their work in 1965 led Ford bigwigs to ask them to handle the pit chores for Jim Clark at Indianapolis. Six of the nine winning cars at Riverside were handled by the team. In 1965 the Woods had winners at Riverside, Indianapolis, Atlanta (twice), Daytona and North Carolina Motor Speedway in Rockingham. During 1967 Cale Yarborough piloted the Wood Brothers Ford Fairlane to two superspeedway victories—the Atlanta 500 and the Firecracker 400.

Banjo Matthews

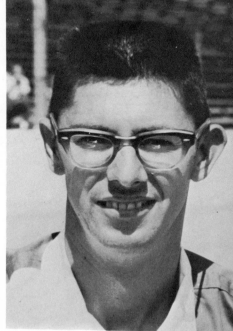

Glen and Leonard Wood

51

Junior Johnson has become quite successful as a car owner and builder since his retirement from the driving ranks. The Rhonda, North Carolina chicken farmer prepared the Mercury and Ford cars driven so successfully by Lee Roy Yarbrough in 1968, 1969 and 1970.

Yarbrough drove Johnson-built cars to two wins in 1968, seven major superspeedway victories in 1969 and two more in 1970. Yarbrough was named Driver of the Year in 1969 by Ford Motor Company, Martini and Rossi and the Southern Motorsports Press Association.

Johnson, famous for his exploits as a driver of Chevrolets, came back in 1971 to build a competitive Chevrolet for the first time since 1963. Johnson's car, with Charlie Glotzbach driving, earned the pole position for both Charlotte races and won a 250-mile event at Bristol.

POINT CHAMPIONSHIP

The Grand National Point Championship is one of the most sought-after laurels in the NASCAR record book. In addition to the honor, it means a sizable chunk of appearance money during the following season. Many winners of the coveted championship have often asked themselves why they tried for the crown, because the grind necessary to earn the title can take a great deal out of both the driver and his equipment.

Names like Lee Petty, Tim Flock, Herb Thomas, Richard Petty, Buck Baker, Jim Paschal, Joe Weatherly and Ned Jarrett show up repeatedly in the NASCAR record books.

Richard Petty and David Pearson are the only active drivers ever to win three GN point championships. The only other driver to accomplish that feat was Lee Petty.

Now retired, Poppa Lee won in 1954, 1958 and 1959 and never finished lower than sixth in the point standings during his 12 years of driving.

Richard won in 1964, 1967 and 1971. In the 14 years Richard has been competing, he has won three times, finished second four times, third twice and fourth once.

Pearson captured his championships in 1966 in a Cotton Owens Dodge and in 1968 and 1969 in the Holman-Moody Ford.

Five others have earned two championships, including Tim Flock, Herb Thomas, Ned Jarrett, Joe Weatherly and Buck Baker. Buck climbed to the top 10 for the first time in 1953, winning the championship in 1956 and 1957, and 10 times in his more than 20 years of racing he has finished in the top 10.

In seven years of competition Ned Jarrett of Newton, North Carolina, won the championship twice and finished in the top 10 in four other years. Little Joe Weatherly, who was known as the "Clown Prince" of racing, won the title in 1962 and 1963, but was killed in the Riverside race in 1964 when his Pontiac slammed into a concrete retaining wall.

Herb Thomas was one of the first seat-of-the-pants drivers to capture the imagination of fans all across the South. One of his championships came in 1953 behind the wheel of one of the now famous Hudson Hornets.

Tim Flock was one of three brothers who took to stock car racing like ducks to water. In 1949 all three were in the top 10— Tim, Bob and Fonty. In 1952 and 1955 Tim captured the title with brother Fonty finishing close to the top.

The point championship requires that a driver make most of the races during the season and finish consistently high. The close races in 1965 and 1966 clearly demonstrate the kind of performance required.

Ned Jarrett and Dick Hutcherson battled it out almost from the start of the 1965 season. Jarrett started 54 races. Hutcherson, driving his first season in NASCAR after three straight years as IMCA champ, entered 52 events.

Hutcherson made it plain that NASCAR didn't frighten him, and he went on to win nine races and finish 37 times in the top 10. But Jarrett proved to be too much for the Keokuk, Iowa, transplant, as he won 13 races, finished second 13 times and compiled 45 finishes in the top 10. Until Jarrett won the Southern 500 at Darlington the point race was nip and tuck, but the cushion this win gave him helped Jarrett wind up the season with a 3,000-point lead.

In 1966 David Pearson and rookie James Hylton battled down to the wire in a race for the championship, which wasn't settled until the last race of the season. Pearson entered 42 races, won 15 and finished 33 times in the top 10. Hylton couldn't make first, but in 41 races he finished 32 times in the top 10.

It was May before Hylton realized that the point chase was shaping up as a battle between himself and Pearson. Hylton started entering every race, and Pearson followed suit. By August, Pearson had built up a 350-point lead, but disqualification at Atlanta cost the Spartanburg driver more than half his edge.

From this point on it was simply a case of a good little guy battling the factory. Pearson had a five-lap lead in the National

500 at Charlotte with the knowledge that, with only one race left, a win would sew up the championship. A blown tire, the fourth one that day for Pearson, put him out of the race and postponed the decision until the American 500. Pearson hung on in the final race of the season and managed a 190-point lead in one of the closest point chases ever.

The drivers compete for other top honors during the season: the most number of wins, the dollar derby, and awards for the Most Popular Driver and NASCAR Rookie of the Year.

Fred Lorenzen set stock car racing on its ear in 1963 when he won the dollar derby with the then-unheard-of figure of $113,000.

Since then, inflation has really set in for the wearer of the dollar derby crown. Richard Petty topped the magic figure in 1967 with earnings of $130,000. Cale Yarborough went him one better in 1968 when he earned $136,800.

Lee Roy Yarbrough earned the title in 1969 with $188,605 and David Pearson finished a close second with $183,700 in earnings.

In 1970 the money was a little more evenly divided, with five drivers earning more than $115,000. Richard Petty was tops with $138,000. Pete Hamilton and Bobby Allison shared second spot with $131,000 each, closely followed by Bobby Isaac with $121,000 and Cale Yarborough with $115,000.

In 1971 Richard Petty became the first driver to win more than $200,000 in a single season. Bobby Allison also topped the $200,000 mark.

James Hylton of Inman, South Carolina, earned the Rookie of the Year award in 1966 by posting the best finish in the point race of any rookie in NASCAR history. Traditionally, rookies who are competing for the Rookie of the Year award will compete strongly in the point race and must finish high.

WATCHING A GRAND NATIONAL RACE

At the start of a Grand National event there is usually a mad dash for the lead. The spectators have little trouble keeping up with the leaders, even after they have lapped some of the slower cars. However, once the cars start making pit stops for fuel and tires or the yellow caution flag comes out, confusion among the spectators is common as they try to decide who is out in front.

An elaborate scoring system is used to keep a record of the cars' progress around the track. Two scorers are assigned to each car. They keep count of the number of times the car passes a certain point. Meanwhile NASCAR officials in the pits record each pit stop.

At the superspeedways the positions of the cars are posted lap by lap.

Transfer of the hastily compiled information from the scorers' stand to the scoreboard and public address system takes some time. At the large tracks records are posted lap by lap. However, at the small tracks, scoreboard records run about five laps behind the actual pace, and changes are posted every five laps.

There is no sure way to tell who is out in front unless you sit in the scorers' stand. But there are a couple of checks that help fans stay abreast of what is going on. When the yellow flag comes out, the caution car will always pick up the leader of the race. There is a catch here, though: the leader is likely to try to take advantage of the yellow flag to make a pit stop while the cars are running at reduced speeds.

Another method of keeping track of the leaders is to watch the blackboard between pit crew and driver. The only way a driver can know what is going on is through his crew's informing him by writing the information on a large blackboard which can be read at a glance from the car. Due to the speed at which a driver passes his pits, his crew will rely on abbreviated instructions. It may be his speed, the number of laps in front or behind, or orders to come in for gas or tires and on which lap to make the stop. Should the pit crew signal in terms of seconds, a quick check of the program time sheet will give the spectator an idea of the car's speed.

In order not to miss the action, spectators should check with track buffs to find out just where the hot spots are. On each track there are one or two places where trouble is most likely to develop. Find out where accidents have occurred in the past and concentrate on those areas. Only rarely will a major accident occur on a straightaway.

There are several signs to look and listen for in order to be on top of the action. Cars going into a turn are more likely to blow an engine as they back off to get through the turn. Although most people expect engines to blow while under strain, usually the opposite is true.

A telltale puff of smoke usually means oil hitting a hot exhaust pipe—or it may be a blown engine. The car may not get into trouble at first, but as the oil hits the track and the rear wheels go over it the car may lose traction. Once tires are slippery with oil anything can happen.

Smoke coming from one of the outside wheels in the turn is not necessarily an indication of trouble. At the speeds the Grand

A member of Cale Yarborough's pit crew holds up a blackboard showing Cale that he completed his last lap in 31.6 seconds.

National cars run, the great pressure exerted on the tires sometimes causes smoking in the turns. In the straights a puff of smoke from the rear may indicate a broken grease seal, leaking rear end or a small oil leak hitting the exhaust pipes.

A blown tire can throw the car into violent gyrations. Blowouts are usually on the outside where the strain is greatest, and a right-front blowout is the most dangerous, since it affects steering.

During pit stops under the caution flag, spectators may have a chance to compare the work of pit crews, as most of the leaders will try to take advantage of the slower pace to take on gas and tires. These pit stops provide an excellent chance to see which car is getting the fastest service, a factor which can play a major role in the outcome of the race.

Pit Stops

A race is often won or lost in the pits, and pre-race strategy is built around the number of stops required during the race.

Each driver and his crew have gone over and over each of the pit stops necessary in the race they are running, barring unforeseen accidents or mechanical failure. Long experience tells the driver and crew just how far he can go on each tank of gas. Tire experts have conducted hundreds of miles of high-speed tests to insure that a driver won't run out of rubber between pit stops.

In a 500-mile race most crews figure on five pit stops, possibly six, since the huge engines drink gas at the rate of approximately one gallon every three to five miles. With a limit of 22 gallons of fuel, the stockers are limited to approximately 70 to 100 miles between gas stops.

During a 30-second pit stop made under the green flag, a car can lose almost a full lap on every track except Daytona. But if a driver can make his pit stops under the caution flag, with the cars slowed down to about 65 miles an hour, he can stop for gas and two tires and be out on the track before the caution car comes back around the track, thus preserving his position. Pit stops will average around 25 seconds for 20 gallons of gas and two outside tires. Very good times range in the low twenties. These are stops without any mechanical problems.

NASCAR rules allow six men over the wall working on the car. One man stands at the front of the pit area to show the driver where he must stop. Should a car go beyond the limits of its pit, then it must continue back onto the track and complete another lap before any work can be done on it.

Each pit crew member has his own specific job and goes about it effi-
ciently with the least expenditure of motion to make for fast pit stops.

The man who stops the car usually goes back behind the pit
wall to make way for working members of the crew. The jack man
is first over the wall, generally in front of the car. At the same time
a man carrying a 10-gallon gas can goes over the wall at the rear of
the car. Crewmen with air wrenches are right behind on either end
of the car.

Two other men follow with fresh tires. As the jack man places
the jack under the outside frame, the gas man is pouring gas into
the filler. The two wrench men have loosened the five lugs on each
outside wheel before the jack man can clear the wheels off the ground.
By the time the right side tires clear the ground, the gas man is
starting on his second 10 gallons of gas.

The instant the tires are off the ground they are pulled free
and replaced with fresh rubber. The wrench man starts tightening
lug nuts as soon as the new wheels and tires are in place.

Assistants grab the old tires as the jack man keeps his eyes
on the gas man and also double checks to make sure all lugs have
been tightened properly. As the gas man dumps the last drops of

fuel into the car, he slaps the trunk. The jack man lowers the car back to the ground, and the driver takes off.

This is the standard plan for a routine gas stop with new rubber on the outside. For stops which require work under the hood, the wrench men must also carry the tires and make the changes so as to free two men to do whatever is necessary under the hood. In the case of changing all four tires in the same stop, another plan is used.

With each car limited to six men over the wall at one time, some of the work must be done by those inside the pit itself. One man may hang over the wall to clean the windshield or hand the driver something to drink. While the work is being done on the car the driver is filled in on how he stands and the strategy for the rest of the race.

The timing of pit stops can be critical. To wait for a caution flag is a pure and simple gamble; therefore many drivers pit on every caution flag for fuel and possibly tires. The yellow flag can be a real blessing to the driver with a minor mechanical problem. A lengthy pit stop can be broken into several shorter ones while the caution flag is out.

While the pit crew works on his car, Darel Dieringer receives instructions from car owner Junior Johnson.

Many a driver has wished he hadn't pitted under the green flag if the caution flag comes out a few laps after his stop, since he might have been able to last those few miles. However, not making stops can prove more costly in the long run. David Pearson, Junior Johnson and Fred Lorenzen all had the same problem in three different National 400s at Charlotte—to pit or not to pit.

Pearson blew a tire with three laps remaining in the 1962 National 400 to pave the way for Junior Johnson's win. Fred Lorenzen gambled and won in the 1964 National 400 when he ran out of gas coming out of the fourth turn and was able to coast across the finish line. In the same race Junior Johnson lost his gamble as he ran out of gas before Lorenzen. The previous year Lorenzen ran out of gas with just a few laps remaining, thereby allowing Johnson to claim the win.

Only minor work can be completed on the car while it is on pit road, but in many cases pit crews have pulled the car behind the wall and replaced rear ends, distributors and other major components in a few minutes. This costs plenty in the way of track position, but in a long distance race anything can happen, leaving the door open as to race strategy.

David Pearson knows what slow pit stops can cost. In 1965 Pearson lost to Dan Gurney in the Riverside 500 by some 90 seconds. A close check of pit stops showed that Pearson spent 140 seconds more in the pits and blew a possible 50-second lead.

Perhaps the best known pit crew in the business is the Wood Brothers. Marvin Panch piloted a Wood-prepared Ford to wins in both events at Atlanta. Dan Gurney captured the Riverside 500 in a Wood-serviced car, and Curtis Turner with the same pit crew com-

When the caution flag comes out, the traffic in pit lane is heavier than it is on the track.

The Wood Brothers wait for their car to come in for a tire change. Glen carries fresh lug nuts as the ones that come off the wheels are too hot to handle.

pleted a comeback to NASCAR racing after a four-year absence with a win in the American 500 at Rockingham. A. J. Foyt appeared in the Firecracker 400 at Daytona in a Wood Brothers' Ford and won going away.

The pits, a mass of tools, spare tires, air bottles, extra parts and oil cans, look like one of the biggest messes ever uncovered in a shade-tree garage. But contrary to appearances, everything is in its place so that the pit crew can get its hands on whatever is needed in the least possible time.

Everyone agrees that a fast pit crew is essential to winning races. Close checks of the time it takes to complete a routine pit stop in practice show whether more dry-run practice sessions are necessary.

Victory Circle

Bedlam reigns in victory circle once the race ends. The driver's crew climbs aboard the winning car and rides into the fenced-off area for a taste of well-deserved glory. Hundreds of fans mill about as cameramen photograph the winner collecting kisses from the beauty queens.

Once the cars have pulled off the track, fans spill out of the stands and infield to catch a glimpse of their hero—sweaty, dirty and tired, but usually willing to say a word or two, sign a program or answer a question. The sun is going down for those who didn't make it to victory circle, but these drivers are already planning for the next race.

WHERE THEY RACE

The Grand National Division competes on a variety of tracks including nine paved superspeedways, two road courses, a series of short paved tracks and dirt ovals from less than a half mile to almost a full mile in length.

The first race of the season is a 500-mile event over the 2.7-mile road course at Riverside Raceway in California. The twisting, tricky track challenges the stockers with right- and left-hand turns, compared to the constant left turns of oval tracks.

The first major test of the season comes in February with the Daytona 500, which usually provides the first real indication of what can be expected during the coming year. A second major event is held at Daytona in July.

Each superspeedway holds two events each year. Atlanta holds a 500-miler in late March or early April and a 500-mile event in August. Darlington schedules a 400-mile race in late April or early May and the Southern 500 on Labor Day. Charlotte hosts the World 600 in May and a 500-mile race in October. North Carolina Motor Speedway in Rockingham holds a pair of 500-mile events, one in June and the other in October. The Alabama International Motor Speedway at Talladega, Alabama holds races of 500 miles in April and August over the 2.6-mile paved course. Michigan International Speedway at Irish Hills, Michigan, hosts two 400-mile events in June and August and Texas International Speedway at Bryan, Texas, hosts two 500-mile events in July and December. Ontario Motor Speedway in Ontario, California, hosts at least one 500-mile stock car event each year as does Pocono International Raceway in Long Pond, Pennsylvania.

Cale Yarborough in victory circle after winning the 1967 Atlanta 500 is surrounded by beauty queens, cameramen and fans.

In between the major scheduled events, the cars are competing on the shorter tracks with asphalt plants at Bristol, Martinsville and North Wilkesboro sponsoring two 250-milers each year and Asheville-Weaverville one 250-miler and one 150-miler.

However, whether it's a short track or a new superspeedway, watching the big stockers roar through the turns and down the straightaways provides thrills and excitement that are unbeatable.

must be of standard production design. Any type rocker arms except ball or bearing types are allowed, unless the special rocker arms are standard on the engines being used. Solid or hydraulic valve lifters are permitted. Roller tappets are not allowed unless standard for the engine being used.

All other NASCAR safety regulations which apply to Grand National cars also apply to Grand American Series cars.

Wheel rims are limited to a maximum width of 8½ inches with a maximum tread width of 10 inches. Cars must start the races on the same tires which are used for qualifying. NASCAR will impound the tires used in qualifying and return them for remounting at the start of the race.

The Grand American cars are required to use the same special safety equipment required of Grand National cars including roll bar cages, seat belts and shoulder harnesses, reinforced suspension, frames, wheels and hubs.

Pit crews on Grand American Series cars are limited to two men over the pit wall at any one time. No car is allowed more than two men except when permission has been granted by NASCAR officials to push start the car. Push start assistance will be limited to five men.

WHERE THEY RACE

Grand American Series races have been held on virtually every size and type of race track, including the road courses at Daytona and Road Atlanta, the superspeedways at Rockingham, Darlington and Atlanta and dirt tracks in Columbia, South Carolina and Richmond, Virginia.

Both qualifying and race record speeds are very close to the records of the Grand National cars. In some cases, particularly on the smaller paved tracks, the Grand American cars are considerably faster than the GN cars. However, on superspeedways and dirt tracks where horsepower and weight are not such a critical factor, the GN cars are considerably faster.

PAST CHAMPIONS

DeWayne "Tiny" Lund of Cross, South Carolina, has achieved a degree of success in the Grand American Series that he was never able to reach in Grand National Competition. The 40-year-old fishing camp operator won the point championship in 1968, finished fifth in 1969 and captured top honors once more in 1970. Lund finished first again in 1971 after a close battle with veteran racer

67

Buck Baker. Lund has won more than 40 Grand American races and collected almost $100,000 in winnings. He won 19 races in 1970, 10 during one hot streak.

The six-foot-four 250-pounder is one of NASCAR's busiest drivers. It isn't unusual for Lund to appear in a Sportsman event, Grand American Series race and GN event all in the same weekend. Tiny is a seasoned Sportsman veteran and a crowd favorite wherever he appears because of his wide-open style of driving.

Ken Rush of High Point, North Carolina, won the Grand American point championship in 1969, although he only managed to win three events during the season. The 40-year-old driver was the picture of consistency, finishing 20 of the 35 races in the top five and six more in the top 10.

Competition during the 1969 series was enhanced by the entry of the American Motors Javelin team with long-time veteran NASCAR driver Jim Paschal handling the driving chores. Paschal won five events and finished in the top five on 12 occasions.

Other top drivers in the Grand American Series include Buck Baker, who has never finished worse than third in the point standings; Pete Hamilton, who won 12 Grand American events in 1969 and has since gone on to become a top money winner in the GN division; and Wayne Andrews, T. C. Hunt, Frank Sessoms and David Boggs.

Mercury Cougar dominated the Grand American Series during the first year with the Chevrolet Camaro and Ford Mustang a very close second and third. Since the initial year, Camaro has dominated the series and piled up a wide point margin. Camaros have won more than 50 Grand American events with Cougar and American Motors Javelin a close second and third. Pontiac Firebird is fourth and Mustang fifth in wins since the division was formed.

In 1970 three veteran NASCAR GN drivers topped the point standings with Lund beating out Jim Paschal and Buck Baker. American Motors Javelin finished second to Camaro in the manufacturer's championship.

THE FUTURE

The future of the Grand American Series is very much in doubt. The division, which was expected to replace the drawing appeal of the GN cars on the shorter tracks, has failed to attract large or consistent crowds.

In 1971, as an effort to bolster the division, NASCAR allowed the Grand American cars to run on the short tracks with the GN

68

cars. The move came after a large number of Grand American races were canceled and the sanctioning body was seeking a way to keep the cars running. This resulted in heavy protests from a number of drivers in the Grand National Division, who complained that the lighter Grand American cars would gain starting positions that should rightfully go to the GN cars in the thick of the fight for the point championship.

As a concession to the GN drivers, NASCAR increased the number of starting positions in events where both GN and Grand American cars are participating.

The plans for the division for 1972 are indefinite at this time. The Grand American Series is expected to continue with separate races wherever possible, allowing the Grand American cars to participate on the short tracks with the Grand National cars.

3

THE LATE MODEL SPORTSMAN CIRCUIT

The Late Model Sportsman Division of NASCAR provides hopeful drivers with the experience needed to go on to the big time on the Grand National circuit and the races with $100,000 in prize money up for grabs.

A medical student faces extra years of preparation before hanging up a shingle to practice medicine. He goes to college, medical school, serves an internship and perhaps a residency before reaching his ultimate goal. For a driver, the Late Model Sportsman Division is similar to a doctor's internship. At this point he has graduated from the $500 Hobby and Cadet cars to the more sophisticated $3,000 to $4,000 Late Model Sportsman. He has served an apprenticeship which included fender banging, trips through the wall, spins and what seemed like tons of red clay.

The Late Model Sportsman Division pays first-place money from $350 to $1,250 in races which range from 40 laps to some 100-mile championship events. Most of the Late Model Sportsman competition is on hard-packed red clay. However, in the major events the scene switches to asphalt.

The Late Model Sportsman Division of NASCAR provides the bread and butter for most short tracks with weekly events. Many Late Model Sportsman drivers compete in three or four races each week. Most weekly events average 40 to 50 laps over tracks ranging from ½ to ⅝ of a mile, making the total distance from 10 to 25 miles. The shorter distances cause less wear and tear on engines, but close competition of 25 to 40 cars going into a 40-foot turn on the short tracks makes sparks fly as fenders wrinkle under contact.

The steady grind of three, four and sometimes five races a week puts a great deal of pressure on the drivers to keep their equipment in good condition, but the lessons learned will serve the driver well if, and when, he moves up to the Grand Nationals.

WHAT IS A LATE MODEL SPORTSMAN?

The Late Model Sportsman cars look basically like the Grand National cars of a couple of years ago. For 1972, no car older than a 1970 model is eligible for GN competition, while the Late Model Sportsman Division is open to cars built from 1960 to 1969. Since the body alterations are pretty much limited to those needed for tire clearance, the Late Model Sportsmen bear a strong resemblance to the cars driven by the spectators. This heightens the association in the fans' minds between their cars and the race cars of similar make, and accounts for much of the growing popularity of the Late Model Sportsman events.

The primary differences between the Late Model Sportsman cars and the Modifieds (other than the eligibility of older cars in the Modified Division) are the NASCAR engine requirements. The Late Model Sportsman cars are limited in engine size and carburetion. They are restricted to 430 cubic inches displacement and one two-, three- or four-barrel carburetor. No overhead cam engines or 1963 Chevrolet high performance 427-cubic-inch engines are allowed.

Any stroke and crankshaft are allowed, provided the cubic-inch displacement does not exceed that specified by the rules. The motor may be moved in the chassis, but the steel firewall must seal the driver's compartment from the engine. Fuel injection and superchargers are forbidden.

Late Model Sportsman cars are required to have a minimum wheelbase of 112 inches with a minimum weight of 3,300 pounds including gas, oil and water. Effective in 1972, this division will be limited to 1960 through 1969 models. There will be no more early model Sportsman cars running with reduced engine displacements. There is a minimum weight requirement of nine pounds per cubic inch of piston displacement. Engines may not be crossed from one manufacturer's line to another. Hemi, high riser, overhead cam engines and heads are not permitted.

While the size of the engines is restricted, there is considerable freedom in what can be done to improve performance as long as displacement stays within the NASCAR rules. Heads may be polished, ported and relieved. Valves may be lightened, and there are no valve size restrictions. High-performance heads are allowed, and interchanging heads in the same manufacturer's line is permitted.

Aluminum and high-performance intake manifolds are allowed. Enlarging and polishing ports in the manifolds is permissible. A special adapter may be used to mount a four-barrel carburetor. Only one four-barrel carb is allowed, including the Holley high-performance model as long as it is properly installed.

PERSONALITIES

Once a Late Model Sportsman car and driver begin to click on a certain track, it may be 10 races before someone can come up with the combination needed to beat the winning team. Dick Hutcherson never lost a Late Model Sportsman race at Monroe, North Carolina, in 1966. While Ford was out of Grand National racing, Hutcherson piled up a string of eight victories in a 1963 Late Model Sportsman Ford.

Ralph Earnhardt of Kannapolis, North Carolina, is the perennial Late Model Sportsman champ of South Carolina and consistently ranks near the top in the national point standings. Earnhardt captured the track crowns at Columbia and Greenville in 1965 and 1966. At one point Earnhardt, who runs at least three times a week, had won so many races at Columbia that the promoter offered a bonus to anyone who could beat him. Earnhardt, like many other drivers, has tried his hand at the Grand Nationals, but prefers the Late Model Sportsman cars.

Tiny Lund, Tom Pistone, Dick Hutcherson, Ned Jarrett, Buck Baker, Lee Roy Yarbrough and Rex White of Spartanburg worked their way up through the ranks, but many are still competing in the Late Model Sportsman Division. Lund, Pistone, Hutch, Lee Roy

Ralph Earnhardt

and many others still make appearances when time permits. Some even return permanently to their first love.

Rex White tasted fame and glory and earned a sizable chunk of change as he pushed his Chevrolet to the Grand National point championship in 1960. He continued on the GN circuit for three years. In 1961 Rex, a fiery little competitor who had to peer over the top of the steering wheel, finished second in the point standings. Again in 1963 he made the top 10, but the withdrawal of Mercury from racing prompted White to call it quits. He couldn't stand being idle when there was racing to do, however, so White resumed driving chores in mid-1964 and 1965, but he joined the Late Model Sportsman ranks. His experience proved worthwhile. In 1965 he finished sixth in the final state point standings in South Carolina and eleventh in North Carolina along with a seventh-place finish in the National Late Model Sportsman point rankings.

LATE MODEL SPORTSMAN CHAMPIONS

Charles "Red" Farmer of Hueytown, Alabama, announced that he was going to take it easy after winning his first Late Model Sportsman championship in 1969. Since then he has taken the 1970 and 1971 titles, competed in more than 250 races and won more than 75 of them. The 22-year veteran driver also won the Modified title in 1956 and was named NASCAR's most popular Sportsman driver in 1969. Red occasionally competes in the rich GN events but depends on races in Huntsville, Birmingham and Montgomery, Alabama, plus special Late Model Sportsman events across the nation for his bread and butter.

Joe Thurman of Rocky Mount, Virginia, was the Late Model Sportsman champ in 1968 after finishing second to 1967 Sportsman king Pete Hamilton.

Hamilton captured his first title in 1967 after four years of trying. The Dedham, Massachusetts, native has since gone on to win GN Rookie of the Year honors in 1968. In 1969, Hamilton switched to the Grand American Division where he won 12 of 26 races he entered.

In 1970 Pete was named to drive the second Petty Enterprises car, in which he captured three major events and earned $131,000. He was named to pilot the American Brakeblok Plymouth, built by Cotton Owens, in 1971.

Don MacTavish of Dover, Massachusetts, won the Late Model Sportsman title in 1966 by winning 28 of 106 races entered. MacTavish finished second on 17 occasions and compiled the remarkable statistic of finishing in the top five 80 times. He was killed in an accident in 1969.

Rene Charland of Agawam, Massachusetts, wore the Late Model Sportsman crown from 1962 through 1965 when he competed in more than 400 races and finished first more than 50 times.

LATE MODEL SPORTSMAN TRACKS

Late Model Sportsman competition ranges from Florida's Daytona International Speedway to Norwood, Massachusetts. The 25 East Coast tracks offer long, short, paved or dirt ovals varying in length from ⅓ to 2½ miles.

Point champions are determined in three areas. Each track has its own champ, and the tracks in each state are lumped into another group to provide a state champion. The national champ does not necessarily hold a state title or even a track championship.

In 1965 Charland won the New York State championship, but didn't capture a single track championship. In 1966 MacTavish finished high in four different states, but couldn't claim a title at any of the tracks.

Virginia boasts four Late Model Sportsman tracks with Alabama, Georgia, North Carolina and Tennessee claiming three each. South Carolina has two, and Connecticut, Florida, Louisiana, Maryland, Massachusetts and Texas each have one. Several Late Model Sportsman tracks operate in California.

On shorter tracks, up to a half-mile, the Late Model Sportsman cars will turn in times just as fast and in most instances a little faster than the Grand National cars and will remain within striking distance of the more powerful Modifieds.

Grand National cars made their first appearance in May of 1966 on Starlite Speedway's .4-mile, high-banked, dirt oval in Monroe. James Hylton set the qualifying mark of 65.099 miles an hour in a 1965 Dodge. Hylton turned the track in 22.37 seconds. Many of the Late Model Sportsman drivers stood in the pits and quietly snickered—for Bunk Moore of Indian Trail, North Carolina, consistently turned the track in 21.5 with a 1963 Ford Late Model Sportsman powered by a 427 CID engine.

The old days of taking a car to every race track on the circuit with the same suspension, engine, gear ratios and tires are gone with the wind. Preparation of Late Model Sportsman cars has become almost as complicated as the Grand Nationals and Modifieds. Sprung weight must be adjusted to each particular track with springs used, type shocks used and adjustments in wedge. The cars must be set up

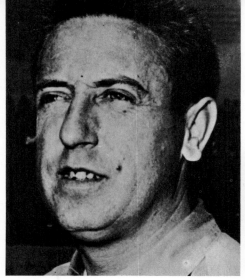

Rex White

Pete Hamilton

Rene Charland

loosely to survive the pounding from dirt tracks but also have to be tight on asphalt to stay out of trouble.

Although many drivers still do much of their own mechanical work, the teams are utilizing more specialists. One may do the engine work while a second handles the chassis setup and the driver coordinates the efforts of both.

Each track has its own secrets and it requires the combined efforts of all the crew to beat it. Jack Smith, a former NASCAR great who now has a chain of transmission shops and a daily racing radio program, maintains that he would rather run one dirt race than a half dozen on pavement. After citing the difference between a wet and a dry dirt track, the Spartanburg ex-driver said, "Racing on dirt is a real challenge because track conditions can change during the race. You may plan to run one way and suddenly you have to adjust to an entirely different situation. It's a shame that the Grand National cars don't run any more dirt races than they do. When I started out in racing, ninety per cent of the races were on dirt."

Certain dirt ovals, where most of the Late Model Sportsman competition is held, gain reputations for being wet or dry. A wet track is one that retains its moisture even in long-distance events, making the track softer than a dry one. Monroe is known as a wet track. Tiny Lund, Bud Moore of Charleston, South Carolina, and Bunk Moore prefer the slick track. "Coming off the corners is easier on the car and driver," Lund explains.

A dry track packs down and dries out to near-asphalt consistency during a race. Columbia, South Carolina, and Hickory, North Carolina, ovals have this reputation. Don Tilley of Statesville, North Carolina, and Sam Smith, of Union, South Carolina, prefer the harder surface. With a dry track there is the problem of switching tires on one of the pit stops due to changing conditions. Many drivers who run 100-milers at Hickory switch to asphalt-type tires as the track hardens.

The Late Model Sportsman Division provides aspiring drivers with an opportunity to learn while doing. Just saying one is a race driver is not enough. It takes years of hard work and plenty of practice to make the title mean anything. Experience is the key, and Late Model Sportsman competition can provide a driver with plenty of that.

THE FUTURE

The emergence of Late Model Sportsman cars will be really felt in the next few years. With the increasing pressure of Grand

National scheduling, more and more demands will be placed on the Late Model Sportsmen to take the place of the small-track Grand National events. If the point race in 1971 was any indication of what fans can look for, then the future should be bright indeed.

The addition of several new superspeedways will place a heavy burden on the Late Model Sportsmen. Longer and richer races for them on the short tracks will have to replace the standard 50-lap feature with a winning purse of $300 to $500.

The trend is already evident. Several major events are scheduled each year at the superspeedways, but the Late Model Sportsmen have not proven to be a major drawing card on the supertracks. Watch for 100-mile Late Model Sportsman events gradually to replace the Grand National events at all but a few dirt tracks and at many of the short asphalt ovals.

4

THE MODIFIED CIRCUIT

For years the Modified Division of NASCAR offered one of the most exciting kinds of racing to be seen. Until 1968 it, like the Sportsman Division, was divided into two divisions, with one just for the late model cars. Then NASCAR combined the Modified and Sportsman cars to form the Modified Division, while moving the Late Model Modifieds into the Late Model Sportsman Division. This move, along with changing trends in racing, has brought about a marked decline in the Modified circuit. In 1967 the Modifieds raced on over 30 NASCAR sanctioned tracks—by 1970 the number had dwindled to a mere dozen. However, many of NASCAR's greats have moved up through this and the other divisions to go on to bigger and better things on the Grand National circuit.

Most Modified pilots run at least three races a week, if they hope to finish well in the national standings. The swift and usually ultra-light machinery competes on tracks in California, Connecticut, New York and North Carolina, and is easily adaptable to either dirt or asphalt.

In the past the Modified cars were allowed virtually any combination of chassis and engine the car builder wanted to use, as long as it conformed to NASCAR rules. There was no limitation on kind of fuel, carburetion, fuel injection, or any other parts for that matter, as long as the car met safety regulations.

Not only did the rules promote wild competition, but they allowed some startling combinations of engine and body. A stream-lined 1954 Studebaker might have had anything under the hood from a 600-cubic-inch full blown Caddy mill to a fuel-injected 327-cubic-inch Chevy engine.

Modified cars had no weight to cubic-inch-displacement requirements, except on tracks north of the Mason-Dixon line where there was a minimum weight requirement of 2,400 pounds for all cars in this division. The displacement was limited only by the width of the cylinder walls before the boring bar struck water.

The trend during the mid-60s was toward the more dependable but smaller engines. The exotic and oversized 400- and 500-cubic-inch engines gave way to bored-out 327s and all sorts of variations of the 352, 383, 396 and even the same engines used to power the Grand National cars.

The advantages of the smaller engines included more durability, easy availability and lower cost without hurting actual performance. On the shorter tracks both Modified and Sportsman cars

All models before 1949 are allowed to run the top portion of the hood without the side portions.

Harold Martin (03) battles Ray Hendrick for the lead in the Modified 300 at Martinsville, followed closely by Perk Brown (45) and Bill Dennis (33).

could outperform the newer Grand National cars by as much as three to six miles an hour.

However, on the longer superspeedways, the superior handling of the Grand National cars made a 10-mile-an-hour difference, and on some tracks even more. Most of the Modified competition even then was on the shorter ovals.

WHAT IS A MODIFIED?

Today the Modifieds are still examples of the results of the builder's nearly unlimited freedom to build performance into a race car. The newer regulations that restrict performance in this division are few. Gasoline is the only allowable fuel now, and multiple carburetion is permitted only on small block engines; otherwise the builder is limited to a single three- or four-barrel carburetor. Fuel injection, superchargers and Holley 4500 series carburetors are not legal. Aluminum blocks are not allowed nor are overhead cam engines unless approved by NASCAR.

Much of this constitutes what a Modified is not. What a Modified *may* be is any make or model 1935 to 1967 sedan type automobile with a factory made steel top, a minimum wheelbase of

109 inches and a minimum weight of 2,600 pounds with gas, oil and water but without driver. The cars must have fenders and running boards, if they were original on the car, and sheet metal missing as a result of an accident must be replaced within two events. As with Grand National cars, all doors must be welded or bolted shut with approved type metal fasteners. A roll-bar cage, a scattershield of at least ⅜ inches over the flywheel and clutch, shoulder harnesses, helmets and other safety requirements of NASCAR must be met.

All pre-1949 models are allowed to run the top portion of the hood without the side portions. All Modifieds are allowed holes no larger than ½ inch diameter bored in the hood for cooling purposes. Any type of ignition system is allowed on the Modified cars, but the self-starter must be in working order. All cars must be able to leave pits and starting line under their own power, but once the race is under way the cars may be pushed off from a pit stop.

Blocks may be bored out to any size, with no displacement limitation. Engines may be interchanged in any manufacturer's line as long as other NASCAR rules are followed. The engine may be moved in the chassis for better weight distribution, but the firewall must separate the driver's compartment from the engine.

Special cylinder heads are permitted as long as they are similar to the original heads. Any stock intake manifold (within a manufacturer's line) may be used. Any type camshaft, valves, pistons and connecting rods are allowed. The fan and fan belt may be removed and the cars may use any type water pump.

The Modifieds are allowed to have the front and rear suspension reinforced and the chassis strengthened as long as the wheelbase remains stock. Coil spring front ends can be changed to straight axles.

Minimum ground clearance for the oil pan will be two inches as determined by removing the left front wheel and resting the brake drum on the ground. (Use of any special device to obtain ground clearance will subject the car to disqualification because such a device may become dislodged while car is in motion, thereby lowering the car below the approved minimum ground clearance.) There may not be any device which allows the driver to shift the weight of the car while in motion.

Locked rear ends and quick change center sections are permitted. Full floating rear axles are compulsory. Heavy duty hubs and spindles are mandatory. Steering must be reinforced. Any type radiator may be used on the cars as long as the hood fits. The cars must have an overflow tank of at least one gallon capacity.

PERSONALITIES

Certain Modified drivers show up regularly in the top 20 each year. Others, who might be just as good but don't have the time to devote to racing, are local track champions. The reign of a Modified Point Champion has been averaging two years with the exception of Bobby Allison of Hueytown, Alabama.

Allison held Modified championships in 1962, 1963, 1964 and 1965 before joining the Grand National circuit full time in 1966. Once a Modified driver always a Modified driver, and Allison that year finished fifth in the national Modified point standings as well as ranking 10th in the Grand National point standings.

Eddie Crouse of Glen Allen, Virginia, and Johnny Roberts of Baltimore, Maryland, each stayed on top of the hill for two years. Two Modified point champs turned the same trick in the Grand National Division after graduating. Red Byron of Atlanta copped the Modified crown in 1948 and then busted the Grand National ranks wide open in 1949.

Joe Weatherly of Norfolk, Virginia, wasn't scared of anything with wheels. He was Modified king in 1953 and Grand National champ in 1962 and 1963. The fiery competitor also held the world motorcycle championship at one time.

Of the current drivers, Clifton "Coo Coo" Marlin of Columbia, Tennessee, is one of the busiest of the new breed. A swift 1966 season at the Nashville Fairgrounds Speedway brought him the track championship. He won 13 out of 15 feature events and decided to try his luck at the big time. In eight days during February's famous

Bobby Allison

"Speedweeks" the thirty-five-year-old farmer raced in the ARCA 250, the Permatex 300 and the Daytona 500. Marlin's wife, Eula, doesn't complain, though. She even admits that his racing efforts have been a financial success, which is a lot more than most can say.

Red Farmer of Hialeah, Florida, now living in Hueytown, Alabama, earned the Modified title in 1956. The wily veteran hasn't slowed down much with age, finishing second in 1965 and 11th in 1966 point standings. Red Foote, a Connecticut Yankee through and through, was 10th in 1965, but slipped out of the top 20 in 1966.

Sonny Hutchins and Runt Harris call Richmond, Virginia, home. Both have been around the Modified circuit for a long time. Hutchins was in the top 10 in 1965 and 1966 and is now tied up with the Wood Brothers, driving their Modified car. He will be one driver in the Modified Division to watch from here on out. Runt has been making left turns in larger numbers than he would want to recall, but it has started paying off. In 1966 Runt worked his way up to 14th in the national point standings.

Friday Hassler of Chattanooga, Tennessee; Carl Burris of Leaksville, North Carolina; Perk Brown of Spray, North Carolina; are all names that have appeared near the top of the final state point standings. Marvin Panch of Daytona Beach, Florida; Donnie Allison, brother of Bobby; Tiny Lund of Cross, South Carolina; and countless others served their apprenticeship in the Modifieds, and many of them still like to take a turn at the wheel of the unlimited bombs. In contrast many Modified pilots have tried their hand at Grand National events but eventually have returned to their first love— the Modifieds.

MODIFIED CHAMPIONS

Carl S. Bergman, better known in racing circles as Bugs Stevens, broke into modified racing in 1966 after one season in Hobby cars and finished second in the point standings to Ernie Gahan of Dover, New Hampshire. The Rehobeth, Massachusetts, driver became the first driver in NASCAR history to win the Modified championship three times, earning the title in 1967, 1968 and 1969. Stevens campaigned a 1964 Ford and a 1937 Chevrolet in 1968 and 1969 losing only one engine in the two years.

Fred DeSarro of Hope Valley, Rhode Island, won the 1970 Modified crown after starting the season without a ride. The 33-year-old driver won 25 of 78 races he entered and finished in the top five a total of 54 times. DeSarro campaigns a pair of 1935 Chevies and a Corvair all powered by 427-cubic-inch engines.

Coo Coo Marlin

Donnie Allison   Red Byron

(L to R) Ray Hendrick, Runt Harris and Sonny Hutchins

Friday Hassler

Perk Brown

Ernie Gahan

Ernie Gahan, a veteran of more than 20 years of competition in the modified ranks, earned the title in 1966 by winning 11 of 71 races and finishing in the top five 49 times.

Jerry Cook of Rome, New York, was runnerup in 1969 and 1970. DeSarro was second in 1968. Ed Flemke of Southington, Connecticut, and "Perk" Brown of Eden, North Carolina, have been consistent finishers in the top five in the national point standings. Cook, Stevens and DeSarro were all involved in the race for the 1971 title.

THE FUTURE

The future is uncertain for the Modifieds as more and more competitors and promoters are switching to the Late Model Sportsman Division. The financial problems of Modified racing are getting out of hand because sheet metal for the older cars is becoming harder to find and more expensive to buy. Also, the wide-open rules policy gives the builders so much freedom to create as they please that they are forced into spending a fortune on modifications in order to remain competitive.

Then, too, many of today's spectators are under 30 years old and cars built in the 30s and 40s aren't easily recognized by them. They find it much easier to identify with the cars that look like the ones they see on the road today. As a result they are more interested in the Late Model Sportsman cars; and what interests the paying public, interests the promoters and the racers.

5

THE LATE MODEL SPORTSMAN SUPERSPEEDWAY CIRCUIT

Prior to 1968 (when the Late Model Modified and Late Model Sportsman cars were combined into a single Late Model Sportsman Division), the Modified-Sportsman circuit combined the talents of more than 900 drivers in both divisions to make for some of the toughest racing competition in NASCAR on tracks ranging from 1½ to 2½ miles.

Late Model Modified and Sportsman cars raced against each other in special events with extra large purses. The points awarded toward the national championship went to each car in its respective division. These major races are held only at NASCAR specified speedways such as Daytona and Talladega and, since the division merger, are open only to Late Model Sportsman cars.

SPECIAL RULES

There are some special rules, which differ from the regular rules for the Late Model Sportsman Division, governing races run on the superspeedways. Before the merger of the divisions, the Modifieds dominated the long-track events because of their unlimited power. The NASCAR rules were changed to allow the Sportsman cars to use hemi and high riser engines in these races which changed the picture a great deal and allowed the Sportsmen to start winning. The merger of the divisions made it no longer necessary to help the

Sportsman cars to be competitive, but in the interests of increased performance on the long tracks the regulations continue to allow the use of hemi and high riser engines. Overhead cam engines and the 1963 Chevrolet 427-cubic-inch high performance engine are still forbidden and the maximum engine displacement remains at 430 cubic inches. Hemi engines are restricted to one four-barrel carburetor with box manifold, while wedge and staggered valve engines are permitted to use multiple carburetion. No fuel injection or superchargers are allowed.

Because of the increased loads placed upon them by the much higher speeds, the front end suspensions must be reinforced and heavy duty spindles and bearings are compulsory. Grand National type Ford front end parts such as spindles, A-frames, steering arms, etc., may be used. Steering parts must be Magnafluxed or Dye-Checked. If found defective, they will be confiscated by NASCAR. No floating type transverse springs are permitted. Stock racing tires with inner safety liners are mandatory and approved oil coolers are recommended.

Safety Regulations

Safety regulations for the superspeedway circuit cars are virtually identical to those which govern the Grand National Division. Roll bars, safety belts and harnesses, helmets, scattershield over the clutch and flywheel assembly and fire extinguishers are required.

One NASCAR rule governing these cars prohibits the use of fins, scoops, wings, air foils and signs in regular competition, but does make provision for use of these special items during speed trials or special tests. All superspeedway events carry a special provision that the top five cars may be impounded and torn down for inspection after the race to make sure they are legal.

THE PERMATEX 300

The season opener at Daytona, preceding the Daytona 500, gives drivers who can afford the long haul to Florida a major jump on the rest of the drivers so far as points are concerned, as well as some $40,000 in prize money.

For years the Permatex 300 attracted many top NASCAR Grand National drivers. With the purse climbing and so many points at stake, more and more Modified pilots were giving up their driving slots to the more experienced Grand National drivers in hopes of having a winning car.

Fords dominated the Modified-Sportsman events at Daytona

Late Model Modified-Sportsman cars racing at Daytona International Speedway during the Permatex 300.

from 1959 through 1966. Banjo Matthews, Tiny Lund, Curtis Turner, Lee Roy Yarbrough, Jimmy Thompson, Marvin Panch and Bubba Farr etched their names in the winner's trophy with big wins in the perennial favorite—Ford.

Jim Paschal changed all that in 1967 when, with three laps remaining, he slipped past Paul Goldsmith's 1964 Plymouth in another hemi-powered Plymouth to take the checkered flag and $7,500 in loot. It started out looking like another Ford sweep, as Lee Roy Yarbrough put his Modified Ford out front and averaged 181-plus for the first nine laps before mechanical problems laid him low. Then it was pole-sitter Goldsmith who led the way.

"Goldie" was a pre-race pick after he set a new record for the Modified-Sportsman cars by turning in a blistering 179-plus qualifying mark. The eligibility of the hemi engines made quite a difference in the performance of the MoPar products, which had been little more than also-rans up to this time.

Then, with an eye toward keeping the Grand National drivers from dominating these events, NASCAR stated that only drivers who

Jim Paschal drives his 1964 Plymouth Sportsman toward victory circle.

regularly competed in the Late Model Sportsman Division would be eligible for the superspeedway races. Since only a few of the Grand National drivers ever ran more than an occasional Late Model Sportsman race, this regulation effectively eliminated the majority of GN drivers from the Late Model Sportsman superspeedway circuit.

PERSONALITIES

Cale Yarborough, who now calls Charlotte, South Carolina, home, is considered one of the top drivers in the GN Division today. He turned down a number of lucrative offers to play professional football so he could race. He was the youngest driver ever to compete in the Southern 500 at Darlington.

In one of Charlotte's Modified-Sportsman events Yarborough crunched his 1956 Modified Ford coming out of the fourth turn during qualifying. He had waited until Friday to try to qualify for the Saturday 250-miler to be sure everything was just right. His brush with the concrete wall demolished the right side of his car. As soon as the wrecker brought his car into the pits, it was loaded and taken back to the shop for repairs.

Yarborough and his crew worked all night to put the car back together and get it running. Just as the starter finished lining the cars up on the track, the Yarborough truck wheeled through the infield tunnel and the crowd came to its feet.

The car was unloaded and placed at the rear of the starting lineup. It wasn't long before Yarborough was battling Lee Roy Yarbrough's yellow Studebaker for the lead. Buck Baker, Perk Brown, Junior Johnson and a half dozen other favorites had fallen by the wayside. Yarborough was cheered just as loudly when he took the checkered flag as he had ever been for a 90-yard touchdown run.

Ray Hendrick and Lee Roy Yarbrough have had their troubles in Modified-Sportsman events. Hendrick and Ernie Gahan were battling for the 1966 Modified point championship right down to the last event of the year, a 250-miler at Atlanta. Hendrick was involved in an accident and finished so far out of contention that he dropped to third place in the final point tally.

Lee Roy Yarbrough came from Columbia to Charlotte in 1965 with his eye on capturing both the National 400 and the Modified 250. Fresh from wins at Bristol and several other major Modified-Sportsman events, Yarbrough earned the pole position and romped off from a slim field of 21 cars.

It appeared as if it might be close once or twice as Carl Burris, Perk Brown and other top drivers challenged during the race, but none of them could stay with the hot 1961 Modified Pontiac driven by Yarbrough. He took the winning flag, only to have a protest filed that one of his rear wheels was too wide. The protest was upheld,

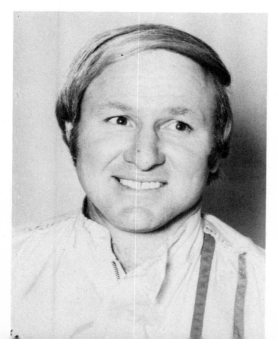

Cale Yarborough

Lee Roy Yarbrough

and instead of first-place money, Yarbrough was left holding the bag. He was the victim of a wrong tire being placed on his car during a pit stop, but ignorance is no excuse.

THE FUTURE

Modified-Sportsman events are just beginning to achieve the popularity they deserve, and for those drivers who have ambitions to step up to the Grand National Division, the Modified-Sportsman circuit provides the final training grounds since the races are held at three of the major tracks—Daytona, Charlotte and Atlanta.

6

THE HOBBY DIVISION

NASCAR's Hobby Division was designed to promote interest in stock car racing by allowing amateur drivers to compete in their own class. It enables those with the desire, but not the financial backing, to participate.

Drivers who have competed in other divisions of NASCAR are not allowed to compete in any of the three classes among which Hobby cars are divided. The Hobby cars are divided into three separate classes, recognizing that there are differences in beginning drivers. The roll-bar cage, seat belts, safety harness and basic NASCAR safety regulations for other divisions apply in all three Hobby classes.

HOBBY CLASS

Cars competing in the Hobby Class may be any American-made automobile from 1936 through 1965. Engine displacement is limited to 335 CID.

Crash bars are allowed on the front and rear of the car, but snowplow-type front bumpers are not legal. Engine requirements include a maximum overbore of .060 inches. Flathead engines are allowed to use multiple carburetion, but overhead valve engines are restricted to one carburetor.

Any grind cam is permissible with the exception of a roller tappet. Supercharging, fuel injection and special intake manifolds are illegal. Fuel cells have been mandatory since January 1, 1968. Radiators must fit in original hood configuration. Floating rear axles are allowed, but not quick-change rear ends.

The suspension may be reinforced, but ground clearance must be maintained at the same levels as in other NASCAR divisions. Only stock transmissions in good working order are allowed. Interchangeable passenger car wheels are allowed, provided they have been reinforced. Heavier hubs and spindles are recommended.

LATE MODEL HOBBY CLASS

Competing models in the Late Model Hobby Class are restricted to 1955 through 1960 American passenger cars. Only Hobby Division drivers may compete.

Engine displacement restrictions for this class are as follows; 1955–57 Fords and Mercurys, 312 CID; 1958–60 Fords, Mercurys and Edsels, 352 CID; 1955–57 Chevrolets, 283 CID; 1958–60 Chevrolets, 348 CID (327 CID engine, heads or intake manifolds are not eligible for the Hobby Division); 1955–57 Plymouths, 301 CID; 1958–60 Plymouths, 350 CID; 1955–56 Pontiacs, 316.26 CID; 1957 Pontiac, 347 CID; 1958–59 Pontiacs, 370 CID; 1960 Pontiac, 389 CID.

Late Model Hobby cars are limited to one four-barrel carburetor. Stock heads, valves and intake manifolds for the engine must be used. HOBBY must be painted on the hood in letters at least 12 inches high. Flywheels and fuel pumps must be stock for the engine being used. Once a driver shows a certain amount of proficiency, NASCAR reserves the right to promote him at any time to the Late Model Sportsman Division.

CADET CLASS

The Cadet Class is limited to inexperienced drivers competing in 1955 through 1964 model American manufactured hardtop passenger cars.

One requisite is use of the standard production engine for the make and model of the car used, using stock stroke and crankshaft. No overhead valve engines are permitted in this class. Everything must be stock in the engine with three exceptions: Any camshaft, except a roller tappet, is permitted; four-barrel carbs are legal, and adapters to accommodate the larger carburetors are allowed.

Cars in the Cadet Class must use approved fuel cells, and all other NASCAR regulations applying to firewalls, filler necks, glass removal and radiators must be followed to the letter. Any stock rear end housing is allowed. NASCAR rules recommend use of floating rear ends. Locked rear ends and any gear ratio are permitted, but quick-change rear ends are illegal.

The rules specify that Cadet cars may have reinforced front or rear suspension. The chassis may be strengthened, but not altered or cut. The same minimum ground clearance rule applies to the Cadets as to all other NASCAR divisions.

With the exception of four-speed manual, any stock transmission in good working order is legal. The rules also allow for the conversion of the steering column three-speed transmission to a floor-mounted shift lever.

Any make tire, original or recap, is allowed. Any size tire is legal as long as all four are the same size. The one exception to this rule allows the left front tire to be one size smaller than the others. Wheel width is limited to 8½ inches.

Dark cars must be lettered in white and vice-versa. All cars must carry numbers between 1 and 99. No letters are allowed, and the identifying numbers must be at least 18 inches high.

LEARNING TO DRIVE IN COMPETITION

NASCAR's Hobby Division is where the men are separated from the boys. The division serves as a training ground for all the other divisions. Cars may cost as little as $150 for the Cadets up to as much as $1,500 for a well-built Late Model Hobby.

Competition is fierce and often frantic as the inexperienced drivers sometimes use each other to stay inside the track as they grind through the turns.

With each race, the drivers gain the knowledge and experience needed to get through an event without bending too much sheet metal. The limited budget of many driving in this division forces the driver to do his own engine and chassis work. As the driver becomes more proficient in his chosen sport, he learns what wedge to put on each wheel. (He may try 10 different spring combinations before he comes up with one that suits him.) Just as each race track has its own favorite route for fast drivers, each driver has preferences about the way his car handles. Three prime examples are Junior Johnson, Richard Petty and Tiger Tom Pistone.

Johnson liked his car's chassis set up tight. He preferred the low grooves to take advantage of the shortest way around the track. To stay low and run fast, a car must be set up with extra stiff suspension. Long and very stiff rear springs are part of the secret, he learned after many years of racing.

On the other hand, Richard Petty likes his suspension set up to allow him to run high if necessary. Most drivers like to stay away from the guard rail, unless they have no choice. However, the advent of safety inner liners has helped eliminate the constant joining of fender and guard rail every time a tire popped. A few other drivers are joining Richard Petty in his all-out quest for the fastest groove.

While heavy duty suspension is a must on every race car, there are degrees of difference. With a race plan which calls for running high, the suspension may not have to be quite as stiff as if the strategy called for sticking to the inside.

While a certain amount of adjustment is necessary for each track, Tom Pistone maintains that the changes need be only minor, except to meet conditions at a couple of superspeedways. He says that by adjusting the wedge, he can run the same race setup on almost every paved or dirt track on the NASCAR circuit.

Similarly, a Hobby driver will soon learn what gear works best in his car. Timing and engine secrets will be revealed every time he makes a mistake. Advice is freely given the beginning driver by competitors in every division. There are very few drivers who won't share the secrets they have learned along the bumpy road.

Action is no stranger to Hobby drivers. Seldom does a 30-lap Hobby race go the distance without a half dozen drivers being involved in some sort of a spin-out. Very few drivers are hurt during these mishaps, because the cars almost invariably are much slower than their big brothers. While the Modified and Sportsman cars can often beat the Grand Nationals around a given track, the Hobby cars, especially the Cadet Class, may be from one to five seconds slower. On a short track those five seconds may seem like an eternity.

TRACKS AND POINTS

The Hobby Division competes on 30 tracks along the East Coast from Georgia to Canada. Drivers are awarded points just as in the other divisions, but there is no national champion. State and local track champions are honored at the end of each season. Limited financing makes traveling up and down the East Coast impractical.

Virtually all Hobby competition is held on tracks where other NASCAR divisions compete on a regular weekly basis. Hobby events at most tracks consist of heat races to qualify for the feature event, with 20- and 30-lap features being the most common. A consistent winner can finance a better car for competition in a higher division the next year, as long as there aren't too many bills along the way. Feature events in the Hobby Division pay anywhere from $100 to win up to $400 for some special 50-lap races.

NASCAR competition has spread from the Southeast through the Northeast with tracks in Massachusetts, Connecticut, New York, Delaware, New Jersey and Maryland. Alabama, Georgia, North and South Carolina, Tennessee and Virginia provide the Hobby thrills in the stock car-oriented southland. While the Hobby races are run as a sidelight to Modified, Sportsman and Grand National events at many of these tracks, this is where the future superstars are gaining the knowledge and experience to one day challenge the kings of the speedways. Although relatively young, the Hobby Division already has produced many Modified and Sportsman drivers, who one day may stand in victory circle at Daytona or one of the other super-speedways.

Racing is a sport that requires tremendous physical stamina, considerable knowledge of innumerable details which go into making a car competitive and above all a desire to race which transcends everything else. Some people see only the glory in the winning car. They fail to recognize that countless hours of preparation went into building the car that took the last spot. Grand National, Modified, Sportsman or Hobby, there is the same amount of blood, sweat and tears underneath that shiny coat of paint.

7

THE WESTERN GRAND NATIONAL DIVISION

In 1954 the National Association for Stock Car Automobile Racing spawned its Pacific Coast Division with ten tracks, most of them in California. Bob Barkhimer of San Jose, California, was the man responsible for the addition of the West Coast Division which incorporates all NASCAR rules and regulations.

Barkhimer's interest in racing dates back to 1937 when he started driving midgets at Alameda and San Francisco. In 1945 he captured the Bay Cities Racing Association championship in northern California and in 1948 was named business manager of the association. In 1949 Barkhimer helped organize the California Stock Car Racing Association with 21 race tracks from Oregon to southern California. That same year he took over management of the San Jose Speedway. From driver to West Coast Regional NASCAR director has been a long and bumpy road for him.

The West Coast drivers compete in the same divisions which attract millions of fans to four times as many tracks along the East Coast, and operate under the same rules.

Competitions in Modified, Sportsman, Late Model Modified and Sportsman Divisions as well as the Limited Sportsman Classes are held weekly at a dozen tracks. The annual Motor Trend 500 at Riverside gives the West Coast boys a chance at the big time money in NASCAR. Few of the drivers are able to take the time or spend the money to come East more than once a year, and only a few make the pilgrimage to Daytona where the rich purse makes the 4,000-mile trip worthwhile.

MARVIN PANCH

A fact not well known on the East Coast is that California has made some major contributions to the world of stock car racing, among them the now retired Marvin Panch, who lives in Daytona Beach, Florida, and works for Grey Rock.

Getting his start back in 1949 with the California Stock Car Racing Association, Panch bided his time and drove as hard as possible while racing in California. The chance to come East arose and he grabbed it. Almost from the minute he arrived Panch was a success in NASCAR circles. In the late fifties, his hard-charging style of driving had attracted a following among race fans and the attention of several top car builders.

Marvin drove anything with wheels in every race that he could get a ride and tied in with Smokey Yunick in 1960. A fast but steady pace in the 1961 Daytona 500 paid off for Panch, as he came home first in one of Smokey's cars. Panch also has wins at Atlanta (two) and Charlotte. His association with the Wood Brothers brought him a certain amount of success, and he improved with each season. In

Marvin Panch

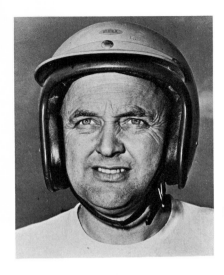

Bill Amick

1964 he placed tenth in the Grand National point standings and moved up to fifth in 1965. With Ford out of racing most of 1966, Marvin bolted the factory team and drove when he could. He switched to a Lee Petty-built Plymouth in the World 600 at Charlotte and outlasted his better-known teammate, Richard Petty, to breeze home the winner and collect more than $25,000. He retired at the end of the 1966 season.

POINT CHAMPIONSHIP

The Western Grand National Division traditionally has one of the closest battles for the season championship.

Bill Amick of Portland, Oregon, who had finished second in the 1964 point standings, earned the title in 1965 by the almost unbelievable difference of six points out of a total of more than 3,000. He edged out Marvin Porter of Torrance, California, in a torrid duel which carried through the final event of the season. Johnny Steele was third, a scant 200 points back.

Things weren't very different in 1966 as Jack McCoy of Modesto, California, ended up on top of the heap by a mere 18 points over Ray Elder, after the final race of the season was canceled because of the weather. Elder and his family had decided to buy McCoy's Dodge after the 1966 Riverside race. Before the car was ready to race a lot of sheet metal had to be unbent in the well-equipped garage on the farm of Elder's father near Fresno. The mechanical crew included the father, Fred; two brothers, Ray and

Richard; a cousin, Ron Koop; and any one or all of a half dozen neighbors who dropped in frequently.

Initially the rookie had no plans for making even the top 10 in the point standings, but in one string of 15 races he managed to finish in the top five a dozen times—and then the contest was on. Ray's wife, Pat, his mother and countless other relatives followed his career closely, right down to the final race in Sacramento.

Both drivers competed in Dodges, McCoy driving a 1966 Charger, and Elder relying on the wedge-powered 1964 model. With only 18 points separating the two drivers, Sacramento's 100-mile Western Grand National over the California State Fairgrounds one-mile dirt track shaped up as a McCoy-Elder special.

It was late in September, but the temperature hovered around

Ray Elder

Jack McCoy

the 100-degree mark as qualifying got underway. McCoy turned in a respectable 42.74-second lap only to have Elder come back with a 42.5 clocking. McCoy brought his Charger back to the line and ripped off 42 seconds flat to set an all-time stock car record.

The race was nip and tuck for the first 60 miles. On lap 62 Elder's engine came apart when a connecting rod let go. Five laps later McCoy was out with a broken wheel bearing. McCoy needed only to finish in front of Elder to clinch the title. With rains canceling the final race at Reno, McCoy was the new champ. He was also voted oval track driver of the year by the Northern California Motorsports Writers and Broadcasters.

Scotty Cain has been in racing for a quarter of a century. The 52-year-old Fresno, California, garage owner won the Western GN point title in 1967 and 1968. Cain started racing in 1946 and has competed in sprints, midgets, roadsters, championship cars and hardtop modifieds. He has finished in the top 10 in the point standings for the past 11 years. He was second, third, fourth and fifth two years each and finished 10th in 1970 at the ripe old age of 50.

Ray Elder is another of the consistent performers on the West Coast Grand National circuit. Elder is the current champ and has held that title since 1969 (three consecutive years). The racing farmer has never finished lower than second in the point standings.

Jack McCoy has had to settle for second place in the standings for the past three years, all because he sold a heavyset farm boy from Caruthers, California a race car. Jack has had trouble beating Elder ever since.

TRACKS AND ACTION

West Coast tracks come in varying lengths and sizes, with some dirt and some paved. The Stockton (California) 99 Speedway boasts a paved quarter-mile oval while the Sacramento track offers a mile of bone-shattering dirt. San Jose, Clovis, Atascadero, Antioch, Champion, Merced, Watsonville and Petaluma Speedways, all in California, host weekly events for the Modified and Sportsman Divisions.

Although there is not as much emphasis on the West Coast stockers, they still provide plenty of action. In 1962 McCoy's throttle stuck as he came out of the fourth turn at Clovis Speedway, and he slammed the wall, demolishing his car. McCoy had another close call at Daytona in 1965 when the Chrysler-powered Studebaker he was driving became airborne and flipped seven times. The car burned, but McCoy escaped with only minor scratches.

One of the most spectacular crashes, according to West Coast buffs, came at Fresno's Kearny Bowl Speedway on May 27, 1966. Steve Bealessio tangled with several other cars coming down the straight at 90 miles an hour. When the car stopped tumbling in the second turn, it had flipped six times and scattered parts and other cars all over the track. Steve escaped serious injury.

THE FUTURE

With the start of 1967 and the promised guidance from the capable hands of Riverside International Raceway's president, Les Richter, prospects look good for a uniform set of rules which will apply to all races. Richter got the green light from Daytona to put into action some plans to create a circuit similar to the Grand National races put on in the East. Admittedly this is a long range goal, eventually to build a circuit carrying equal prestige and with purses much closer to those offered on the East Coast.

One of the first steps toward organization was the hiring of permanent officials who operated on a budget from Daytona. Ken Piper served as the first chief steward with Pete Keller taking over. Piper has recently been re-assigned to the Western Grand National Division as director.

In harmony with building a prestige circuit, the West Coast has been divided into three areas to encourage a stronger Modified-Sportsman "feeder" program. These areas are Northern California, Southern California and Arizona, and Washington and Oregon.

More new cars are being seen on the West Coast each year and Ray Elder's victory in the 1971 Riverside 500 gave the Western Grand National Division more prestige and recognition than ever before.

8

THE PAVED SUPERSPEEDWAYS

DARLINGTON INTERNATIONAL RACEWAY

Darlington International Raceway is the "Granddaddy" of NASCAR superspeedways and as much a part of southern tradition as grits and red-eye gravy. Located just west of Darlington, South Carolina, in the heart of cotton and tobacco land, the toughest and oldest superspeedway dates back to the early days of NASCAR and represents the optimism of the early backers of stock car racing. A group of local citizens organized a stock corporation to build a major speedway in 1949. December 13, 1949, ground was broken on a 70-acre site for a 1¼-mile paved track and a 9,000-seat grandstand. The first race was scheduled for Labor Day 1950. It was slated to be a 500-mile event for stock cars. The race was named the Southern 500.

The First Race

People who were close to automobile racing laughed at the idea of stock cars racing for 500 miles. Sure, there had been some long-distance endurance tests for automobiles, but never an all-out 500-mile race over a closed oval track. Despite serious doubts concerning the success of such a foolhardy venture, the Central States Racing Association and NASCAR agreed to sanction the race with a $25,000 purse. Track officials were hopeful that they could draw a crowd of 10,000.

Johnny Mantz won the first Southern 500 in 1950 by a margin of more than 11 miles over the second-place car.

Race day drew near, and the attention shifted from cotton, tobacco and sweet potatoes, which dominate the long hot summer months in that state, to the boldly conceived idea of racing automobiles for 500 miles over the unchristened race track.

A field of 75 cars started the first race as 30,000 people jammed every available foot of space. There were Lincolns, Mercurys, Hudsons, Oldsmobiles, Nashes, Plymouths, Studebakers, Buicks, Cadillacs and a couple of Kaisers. Wally Campbell earned the pole position in a 1950 Olds with a qualifying speed of 82.35 miles an hour.

By today's standards the race was comic. Many of the cars were driven to the race track, and several used more than 30 tires to go the distance. When the smoke had cleared, Johnny Mantz, whose Plymouth started in forty-third position, was declared the winner. His margin over the second-place car was more than 11 miles.

Mantz, who never had won a NASCAR race before—nor did he again—had taken advantage of an offer from Firestone to try out some new tires, developed with asphalt racing in mind. While others sat in the pits replacing tire after tire, Mantz piled up an ever-increasing lead. Red Byron, a NASCAR great even at that early stage, was the only driver in the first 15 starters to finish the race.

But they had done it. They had staged a 500-mile race for stock cars, had drawn a field of 75 entries and a crowd of 30,000 in the face of advice from the experts who said it couldn't be done— and this was just the beginning!

Expansion and Growth

Between the 1952 and 1953 races the first turn was rebuilt, making the track 1⅜ miles rather than the original 1¼. With the increased length, speeds began to climb. Fonty Flock burned up the track in qualifying his 1953 Hudson Hornet with an average speed of 117.4 miles an hour, but the laurels went to Buck Baker in the first of three wins at Darlington for the Charlotte grandfather. Buck brought his 1953 Olds home first at an average speed of 92.78 miles an hour, almost 20 miles an hour faster than Fonty Flock's winning average in 1952.

New grandstands were also built, raising the seating capacity to its present total of more than 39,000 on the front- and backstretches, with room for another 40,000 in the infield. Attendance figures have soared as high as 75,000 for the Labor Day event, which has long been a stock car racing classic.

Race week in Darlington combines the pageantry of parades, a beauty contest, a golf tournament and a colorful pre-race show. While the Labor Day weekend is traditionally the last weekend to hit South Carolina's Grand Strand beaches, race fans head to Darlington. The population swells from the normal 6,500 to ten times that number.

Buck Baker's Oldsmobile in which he won the 1953 Southern 500 can now be seen in the Joe Weatherly Museum.

One of Bud Moore's Mercurys limps home during the 1965 Rebel 300. Scenes like this are everyday occurrences at Darlington.

The track infield becomes one giant carnival the night before the race as thousands of fans arrive early to camp in their favorite spot. Combos, camp fires, and the party atmosphere all combine to add to the excitement as the sun peeps over the guard rail in the fourth turn.

The tension mounts as the sun climbs higher. The drivers' meeting ends under the slight protection of an inspection shed. The huddle of drivers heads for the concession stands and a cool drink before the hot, grueling challenge of the Southern 500 gets underway with the traditional starter's call of "Gentlemen, start your engines."

Rebel 400

In 1957 Darlington added a second race to its annual schedule, the Rebel 300. The race was set for the Saturday nearest Confederate Memorial Day, May 10. The race was originally intended for the Convertible Division. When the Late Model Convertible Division was eliminated in 1960 because of growing interest in the Grand National Division, the Rebel 300 was retained and made a regular Grand National event.

In 1963 the late president of Darlington, Bob Colvin, devised the idea of splitting the race into two 150-mile races with a Le Mans type start. Joe Weatherly won the first half and Richard Petty took the second 150-miler, but Weatherly was declared the overall winner.

In 1966 the Rebel 300 was lengthened to 400 miles, and Richard Petty wrote his name in the Darlington record books as a winner. Neither of the Pettys had made it to victory circle there before. Lee Petty competed in 11 Southern 500s, his best finish being sixth in the 1952 race. Poppa Lee started four Rebel 300s before he retired and compiled a much better record in this race with a fifth in 1957 and a fourth in 1960.

Richard, however, has a much more enviable record, although he can't shake the fates in the Southern 500. Since 1959 he has finished third, fourth, fifth and sixth in the Labor Day event and owns two seconds, a third and two big wins in the Rebel 400 (1966 and 1967).

Petty's luck changed in the Southern 500 in 1967 establishing a record of 130.423 miles an hour for the distance, which still stands today.

The Darlington Stripe

None of the drivers will argue that Darlington's tricky 1⅜-mile course is the hardest track to get around on any given day. It isn't as fast or as long as most of the other superspeedways, but as Curtis Turner says, "You really have to do some driving here. It takes more wheeling to get around it."

While leading the 1958 Rebel 300, Eddie Pagan missed the groove and crashed through the guard rail. He didn't get a scratch in this wreck!

Bub Strickler puts on a show for the press during the 1965 Rebel 300.

Darel Dieringer's Ford catches fire after a brush with Bobby Johns (72) during the 1962 Southern 500.

Sam McQuagg and Richard Petty dangled their feet off the rear fender of Petty's car in the garage area. McQuagg was a virtual newcomer to Darlington and there were some questions he wanted answered before he took his life in hand and went out to qualify.

"I've run as much practice as I can since we got here, but the track seems different every time I go around," McQuagg said. "What's the best way to get around this track, Richard?"

The tall, smiling Petty shrugged his shoulders in a palms up gesture and answered, "When you find out, let me know."

Some drivers fear Darlington, others hold it in awe. Curtis Turner would rather drive at Darlington than at any other race track, but every driver who has ever raced here respects it. The low and almost flat approaches to the turns make negotiating them at top speed dangerous at best, and hazardous with a tiny slip.

Darlington's turns are mostly one high-speed groove which the drivers must take if they hope to get through as fast as their equipment will take them. Passing is possible in the first and second turns, but only if the leading car makes a mistake by either drifting high or undershooting the turn. Down the backstretch a driver can make his move, but it must be quick because there is only one way through the third and fourth turns.

And then, in order to take full advantage of the big circle, a driver must put the right side of his car up against the guard rail in the third turn to keep the rear end in shape. This contact with the guard rail soon taught Darlington race fans that the "hot dogs" always scratched the paint on the right side, or they weren't pushing their cars to the limit. And the only way to win at Darlington is to shoot the works.

The missing paint and bent sheet metal soon earned the nickname of "The Darlington Stripe" for the fast third turn, and drivers who don't display the well-worn purple heart are looked on with disdain.

Action

No race fan will admit that he travels to NASCAR races for the blood and gore which sometimes accompanies a real fender-banging duel. The present speeds on the supertracks forbid much dueling of this sort, but every once in a while a miscalculation or error in judgment will result in a grinding crash. Inexperience, fatigue, mechanical troubles—all contribute to the problems which can develop. Darlington has been the scene of more spectacular accidents than any two other tracks.

In 1958 Eddie Pagan earned the pole position in the Rebel 300. Pagan's lead was short-lived as he missed the groove and ploughed up a goodly portion of the guard rail in the process. Despite demolishing his 1958 Ford, Pagan walked away from the accident without a scratch. However, he never ran at Darlington again.

In the 1965 Rebel 300, Bub Strickler got a wheel up on the retaining wall as he went into the first turn, rolled over and went through the first and started into the second turn upside down. His 1964 Ford smacked the guard rail in front of the press box. Strickler climbed from his car with only a few cuts and bruises and came back for the Southern 500.

In the 1965 Southern 500, Cale Yarborough and Sam McQuagg touched fenders as Yarborough tried to pass McQuagg in the number one groove. Cale's Ford climbed over the front of McQuagg's car and came to rest against a light pole outside the guard rail. Cale was unhurt.

In 1966 Earl Balmer provided the thrills in the Southern 500 when he and Richard Petty tangled going into turn No. 1. Petty made it, but Balmer rode the guard rail all the way through the turn, almost ending up in the press box. He suffered a small cut on his knee.

Darel Dieringer was snakebitten by the "Lady in Black" for years here. In the 1962 Southern 500, Mamie Reynold's Ford caught fire after a brush with Bobby Johns' Pontiac. Darel had to scramble out in a hurry. The Charlotte, North Carolina, driver overcame his problems with lady luck and came home a winner in the 1966 Southern 500 driving Bud Moore's Mercury Comet.

Two of the more spectacular crashes at Darlington have involved two of stock car racing's most famous drivers, Richard Petty and Fred Lorenzen.

Petty's accident occurred during the 1970 Rebel 400. Coming off the fourth turn, Petty's Plymouth slammed into the outside wall and then headed for the concrete retaining wall which separates the track from pit road. Before 40,000 horrified spectators the car rammed the retaining wall, turned end over end and then rolled sideways with Richard's arm hanging from the driver's window. Richard escaped with a dislocated shoulder and was able to return to driving after about six weeks' recuperation.

Lorenzen wasn't quite so lucky. Driving the Wood Brothers Mercury in preparing to qualify for the 1971 Southern 500, Lorenzen suffered a broken ankle in a similar accident. Fred lost control coming out of the fourth turn, rode the wall for almost half of the front stretch and crashed head-on into the concrete pit wall. Two drivers and two tire company employees pulled Lorenzen from the flaming wreckage. He had several broken ribs, a crushed ankle and lacerations—a small price to pay for a 140-mile-an-hour crash.

Joe Weatherly Museum

Bob Colvin, a prime mover in the rapid rise of Darlington, conceived the idea of the Joe Weatherly Museum shortly after Little Joe died at Riverside, California.

The $100,000 museum opened in May of 1965. It houses many of the cars which have won at Darlington as well as stock car racing's Hall of Fame. Johnny Mantz's 1950 Plymouth, Buck Baker's 1953 Olds, Fireball Roberts' 1963 Ford, manufacturers' displays and other artifacts, including working models to explain the operation of a stock car, are on display. The museum is open to the public free of charge, and more than a million visitors have passed through the modern brick building which stands in the shadow of the front-stretch grandstands.

Personalities

Glenn "Fireball" Roberts heads the list of Darlington winners with four trips to victory circle, two in each of the races. Herb Thomas and Buck Baker own three wins each, all in the Southern

500. Thomas won in 1951, 1954 and 1955. Baker spread his victories out with one in 1953, another in 1960 and the third in 1964.

Curtis Turner, Nelson Stacey, Joe Weatherly and Fred Lorenzen have two wins each here. Turner and Stacey have won in the Southern 500 and the Rebel 300, while both Weatherly's and Lorenzen's wins came in the Rebel 300.

Darlington is noted for close finishes. As a matter of fact, Junior Johnson of Rhonda, North Carolina, went home the winner of the 1962 Southern 500, only to find out the next day that he actually finished second to Larry Frank due to a scoring error. Johnson drove his Ray Fox Pontiac into victory circle, collected kisses from beauty queens and accolades from the throngs pushing and shoving to get a closer look. But a recheck of the scoring sheets later showed that Frank had not been credited with one lap, which put the Greenville, South Carolina, driver out in front.

The 1961 Rebel 300 featured a fender duel between Curtis Turner and Fred Lorenzen which ended with the young driver showing the "old pro" a trick or two. With some 20 laps to go Turner and Lorenzen dueled bumper-to-bumper in a lap by themselves, with first one and then the other grabbing the front spot. Turner, never one to shy away from a little contact, bumped Lorenzen as the cars flashed through the first and second turns. There was more contact as the closing laps wore on.

Lorenzen grabbed the lead with two laps to go and positioned his car smack in the middle of the track to effectively block Turner's effort to pass. Some say that Turner got a dose of his own medicine. Afterward neither would admit that it was anything more than the heat of competition, but those who witnessed the final moments will always wonder.

DAYTONA INTERNATIONAL SPEEDWAY

The hard sands of Daytona Beach have hosted the fastest racing cars in the world since the turn of the century. Such names as Ralph DePalma, Tommy Milton, Ransom E. Olds, Henry Ford and Barney Oldfield are etched in the sands, never to be washed away by time or tide.

Alexander Winton established the first record of 68.198 miles an hour along the deserted, hard, white sand. William K. Vanderbilt, Fred Marriott and the British speed king Sir Malcolm Campbell wiped out this mark and went on to faster times. Sir Malcolm pushed the record to 276.816 before the Atlantic beaches were forsaken for the salt flats of Utah. But after the exodus of the land speed record drivers came to the road course over the beach and several paved streets, where Late Model stock cars, the Modifieds and the Convertibles battled for the prestige of winning at Daytona.

The city of Daytona Beach sponsored the first two races run over the old beach course. A tall, gangling driver from Horse Pasture, Virginia, named William Henry Getty France was one of the drivers in the 1936 and 1937 races. In 1938 Bill France took over promotion of the annual event which attracted thousands along the sprawling course. For France it was the beginning of a promotional career which has yet to reach its peak.

The beach course races were discontinued during World War II, but Bill France renewed the classic in 1946 and helped bring some order to stock car racing with the organization of the National Association for Stock Car Auto Racing. NASCAR grew and the popularity of the beach competition grew beyond the capacity of the course. Tides, too, created problems which no one could control, occasionally forcing postponement of races, so in 1958 ground was broken for the 2½-mile Daytona International Speedway on a 450-acre site near Daytona Beach.

The giant racing plant is almost a city within itself. Facilities include a fully equipped hospital, cafeteria, carpenter shop, paint shop, control tower, scoring stands, permanent service buildings for accessory firms, covered inspection areas and countless rest rooms.

The Speedway's offices as well as NASCAR headquarters are located on the premises. Six grandstands accommodating 50,000 racing fans surround the high-banked asphalt track, and parking space for 50,000 cars is available in the infield.

When the gates opened in February of 1959 for the first Speed Weeks at Daytona, Bill France finally had a dream track impervious to the winds and tides which had played havoc with the beach course. It was the start of an era in stock car racing, which saw superspeedways spring up all across the Southeast with more to come in other sections of the country in the near future.

Track Layout

The Daytona layout was designed for high speed and a variety of types of racing. The main track, 2½-miles in length, is designed with a straight backstretch but the front chute is bowed out, giving the track a D-shape. The front or homestretch is called a trioval, having two slight bends which give the track three turns. The turns are banked 31 degrees and the trioval has an 18-degree bank. The infield includes a 3.81-mile road course which is used for national and international sports car events and motorcycle races.

During its brief history Daytona has become one of the busiest racing plants in the world. The entire month of February is filled with stock car and sports car racing events.

The Daytona Continental started out in 1962 as a three-hour race and has grown into one of the major sports car events in the world. In 1964 the event was lengthened to 2,000 kilometers and, in 1966, to a full-scale 24-hour endurance test. During the latter weeks of February, Daytona hosts a 250-mile race for the Automobile Racing Club of America, a 300-mile Modified-Sportsman race (Permatex 300), a pair of 125-mile qualifying races for the Daytona 500 and finally the 500-mile prestige loaded race which carries a purse in excess of $200,000. Daytona hosts a 400-mile NASCAR race July 4 and in 1967 instituted a 250-mile race, sanctioned by the Sports Car Club of America.

SCCA regional races are held each year in August or September, and the SCCA's annual American Road Race of Champions is conducted in alternate years in November.

Meanwhile the NASCAR Drag Racing Division has taken over the Deland (Florida) Airport and the odor of burning nitro permeates

An aerial view of the front stretch, which is called the trioval because of the curved area in front of the pits, at Daytona International Speedway. The lead cars are heading into the first turn.

the air along with the smell of burning rubber as the NASCAR drag season opener in February attracts top drag racers.

Races and Personalities

Only one man can claim four victories at the Big D; two others own three wins apiece and one other owns two first-place finishes.

The late Fireball Roberts won the Daytona 500 in 1962 and the Firecracker 400 in 1959, 1962 and 1963.

Cale Yarborough of Timmonsville, South Carolina won the 1968 Daytona 500 and owns back-to-back victories in 1967 and 1968 in the Firecracker 400. Cale is the only man ever to win three consecutive races at Daytona.

Lee Roy Yarbrough won the 1969 Daytona 500 and the Firecracker 400.

Richard Petty owns three victories which all came in the February classic. Richard accomplished the feat in 1964, again in

An aerial view of the Grand National stockers going through the second 31-degree banked turn.

Darel Dieringer leads the pack coming out of the fourth turn and onto the main straightaway.

1966 and in 1971. He and his father own a total of four wins, with Poppa Lee's victory coming in the first race staged at Daytona in 1959 in one of the most exciting finishes ever recorded in a stock car race.

Cotton Owens was the fastest qualifier with a speed of 143.198 miles an hour in a 1958 Pontiac. The advantage didn't last as Bob Welborn of Greensboro, North Carolina, shot into the lead on the first lap.

Seven men led the first race, with a total of 34 lead changes in the 200-lap event. Tom Pistone, Jack Smith, Joe Weatherly, Fireball Roberts, Johnny Beauchamp and Lee Petty shared the lead during the long afternoon. The race was half over before Beauchamp and Petty moved into contention, but it was almost three days after the race before anyone knew for sure who had won.

Petty's 1959 Olds and Beauchamp's 1959 T-Bird exchanged the lead 11 times during the last 50 laps, and the cars crossed the finish line side-by-side. There was no camera at the finish line because no one dreamed that a field of 60 cars could start a 500-mile race and have two cars cross the finish line at the same time.

Quick checks of photos and movies of the tremendous finish left some doubt. Petty fans screamed that he had won, and Beauchamp supporters shouted just as loudly in his corner. Finally a photo was found which showed the two cars crossing the white stripe which meant the difference between first and second. It showed Petty's Oldsmobile out in front by a mere four or five inches.

All the races at Daytona haven't been quite that exciting, but

Richard and Poppa Lee in the winner's circle after Richard won the 1966 Daytona 500.

there have been some real storybook finishes. Almost every 500-mile event has seen at least two cars and sometimes as many as four in the same lap when the checkered flag fell. None of them has been quite as close as the first one, but there have been several times when the race was decided by a daring pass on the last lap.

Tiny Lund got an unexpected break in 1963, and almost as if it had been written for a television script, the 270-pound driver won the Daytona 500. A few weeks earlier Marvin Panch's Maserati had rolled over during practice runs for the Continental. Tiny was one of the men who pulled Marvin from the burning car just in time to save his life. With burns over about 40 per cent of his body, "Pancho" asked that Tiny be allowed to drive his Ford in the 500.

Starting from the 12th spot Tiny drove a steady race. So steady in fact, that by the 350-mile mark he, Fred Lorenzen and Ned Jarrett were in a lap by themselves. The three Ford hotshots exchanged the front position 11 times during the late stages of the race, with Tiny going out in front for good on lap 193 to collect more than $25,000.

Richard Petty just about decided to quit running Daytona in the odd-numbered years. In his first start in 1959 he finished 57th.

In 1960 he improved enough to gain the third spot. In 1961 Poppa Lee went over the wall and spent some 40 days recuperating. Neither Petty finished. In 1962, with his father on the mend, Richard finished a strong second in what was considered sadly inferior equipment. He made his best odd-year showing in 1963 when he managed a sixth place.

The 1964 event was run in record time due to the blinding speed of the hemi engine, and Richard romped home first by more than a lap over Jimmy Pardue in another Plymouth. It was the only race of 500 miles at Daytona in which there weren't at least two cars in the same lap at the finish.

Chrysler sat out the 1965 season because of a dispute over the hemi engine. Richard Petty didn't even compete. In 1966 Chrysler and Richard came back to take his second win. The race was stopped after 495 miles because of a Florida rainstorm which threatened to drown the seagulls watching the race.

In 1967 "Poor Richard" was bound and determined to break the jinx which had stopped him short in every previous odd-numbered year. Bound and determined was about all, though. The Plymouth he drove was involved in a minor bump-up early in the event, and the rear wheels were knocked out of line. He had to spend far too much time in the pits to hope to finish out front, but he still managed an eighth-place finish. The Pepsodent Kid, a nickname earned by his wide friendly smile, said his pit crew didn't tell him how badly his car was damaged or he might have parked it.

It took Richard 13 years to break the odd-numbered-year jinx at Daytona. Richard edged out teammate Buddy Baker in a Dodge and A. J. Foyt in the Wood Brothers Mercury to climb to the top of the list of money winners at the track.

Although Petty has never won the Firecracker event, he finished second in the 1971 July 4 event with teammate Baker a strong third.

Closed-Circuit TV

Daytona International Speedway took another giant step toward comprehensive promotion of stock car racing in 1967 when the Daytona 500 was shown across the United States, in Canada and overseas on closed-circuit television.

While almost 100,000 race fans shivered in unseasonably cool weather in sunny Florida, another 200,000 people sat back in their hometown theaters and watched one of the most thoroughly covered races ever broadcast live.

The Indianapolis "500" has been televised for several years,

119

but this was the first time a stock car race had been presented on such a wide distribution basis. It was a smashing success both financially and in enhancing the sport for those not able to travel to Florida.

ABC television began selected showings of stock car races live in 1970. Races had been taped by Wide World of Sports and telecast on a delayed basis up until that time and the network has since returned to the taped format. During the first year of live race broadcasts little or no action occurred and in many instances when something did happen, the cameras were focused on the leaders and missed the action entirely.

Additional money has been added to the purses through the sale of television rights.

Prize Money

The drivers benefited from the TV coverage by the addition of some $25,000 in prize money. Total posted awards exceeded $192,000, and additional lap money and other awards pushed the figure over the $200,000 mark. Mario Andretti pushed his 1967 Holman-Moody prepared Fairlane across the finish line first to collect $43,500—the largest first-place prize ever paid in a NASCAR event.

Only four NASCAR drivers were able to top that figure during the entire 1966 racing season—Richard Petty, David Pearson, Darel Dieringer and Paul Goldsmith. No one else even came close. Fred Lorenzen became the first driver ever to win more than $100,000 in a single season when he earned $113,000 in 1963.

Richard Petty and Bobby Allison accomplished a feat thought to be impossible only five years ago. Both won more than $200,000 in a single racing season (1971). Buddy Baker and Bobby Isaac both topped the $100,000 mark in 1971.

In 1970 five drivers earned more than $100,000. They were Richard Petty, Bobby Isaac, Bobby Allison, Pete Hamilton and Cale Yarborough. Five other drivers earned more than $50,000. They included James Hylton, David Pearson, Charlie Glotzbach, Buddy Baker and Benny Parsons.

In 1969 Petty, Pearson and Lee Roy Yarbrough topped the $100,000 mark. Pearson and Cale Yarbrough passed the magic figure in 1968 and Petty topped $100 grand in 1967.

Driving the Big D

With the rapid increase in speeds, driving Daytona's 2½-mile oval has become more difficult with the years. When the track opened in 1959 the top qualifying speed was just over 143 miles an hour. In

Curtis Turner, fastest qualifier for the 1967 Daytona 500, blows his engine on the front stretch.

qualifying for the 1967 Daytona 500, Curtis Turner of Charlotte drove Smokey Yunick's Chevelle to a new record of 180.831 miles an hour. On the 16th lap of the race Buddy Baker set a new record for stock cars in competition, when his Ray Fox-built Dodge Charger posted a speed of 182-plus.

Cale Yarborough holds the current qualifying record at Daytona set February 22, 1970 in the Wood Brothers 1969 Mercury with a speed of 194.015 miles an hour.

Introduction of the carburetor restrictor plate and sleeve cut speeds back to the 185- to 187-mph bracket in 1971.

The art of drafting was developed at Daytona to increase speeds and at the same time save fuel. Drafting is the trick of moving one car to within inches of the car in front so that the vacuum created by the first car pulls the second car along. At the speeds these cars now travel, air passing over the rear of a car creates a small vacuum pocket just behind the car. If the following driver can get the front of his car into this pocket, the air passes over both cars, and the front car does most of the pulling.

Up to 170 miles an hour, it is possible to break the draft without creating a hazard to either car, but once the speeds approach 180 miles an hour, one driver can force the other to stay in position as long as the draft is maintained. The advantages belong to the

121

driver in the rear. His speed as well as that of the front man is increased, but the back man can force the front car to continue around the track even when the front driver heads for the pits.

There is no special groove around the Big D. The track is wide enough for the cars to travel four abreast at virtually any point. Speeds down the 4,000-foot back chute approach 200 miles an hour. With the average speeds approaching 180 miles an hour the cars are traveling 264 feet per second. While it might take a man 50 minutes to walk around the inside of the track, a race car will travel the same distance in 50 seconds.

At these speeds there is little room for error. The slightest miscalculation could be disastrous. Safety precautions have been improved considerably. When Richard Petty and Earl Balmer tangled at 178 miles an hour during the 1966 Firecracker 400 both drivers escaped with minor bruises, although both cars were demolished.

Each driver seems to have his own particular groove at Daytona. Petty likes the high road. Junior Johnson always seemed to favor a much lower slot, while Goldsmith and many other drivers

The science of drafting was never more excitingly displayed than it was during the 1971 Daytona 500 as 11 drivers swapped the lead a record number of times—48. At the moment this picture was taken, eventual winner Richard Petty was in third place behind Pete Hamilton and Buddy Baker, and ahead of Bobby Allison and Richard Brooks.

stick fairly close to the middle of the race track except when trying to get around slower moving traffic.

As at every other race track, a driver must have some preconceived plan of action based on what he thinks will happen during the race. Pit stops, tire changes and every other factor must be taken into consideration. Strategy, more often than a heavy foot, puts the driver in victory circle.

Fred Lorenzen used a special strategy to win a qualifying race in 1967 by completing the entire 100 miles on a single tank of gas. He established a new record of 174.583 miles an hour for a 100-mile event. It worked so well during the qualifying race that he decided to use the same trick in the 500-miler. Gambling that there would be very few pit stops, Lorenzen geared his car higher to get better gas mileage. Unfortunately for him, the yellow flag was out nine times, meaning gas mileage was relatively unimportant.

Andretti took over the lead in the latter stages of the race with Lorenzen the only other driver in the same lap. Lorenzen was drafting Tiny Lund's Plymouth, but because of the higher gear ratio he couldn't break the draft, and undoubtedly he wouldn't have caught Andretti if he had been able to get around Lund. Lorenzen's strategy backfired, and he economized himself right out of the winner's circle.

Much careful consideration is given to each part that goes into the cars which run at Daytona. A bit of Chrysler strategy in 1966 made Sam McQuagg very happy. Driving a Ray Nichels-built Dodge Charger, Sam showed up at Daytona for the July 4 Firecracker 400 with a spoiler on the rear deck. It was a regular option on the Charger and ruled legal.

Shaped much like an air foil or airplane wing, the Charger left a lot to be desired as a race car. However, the addition of the spoiler made the Dodge so competitive that Sam won the 400-miler going away.

The Future

With tire improvements and mechanics squeezing every ounce of power out of engines, speeds will continue to climb at Daytona unless stringent engine restrictions are imposed. Since this is not very likely, other stabilizing features can be expected to be legalized to help keep the stock cars from becoming airborne.

The NASCAR rules permit a fixed spoiler on all cars, and use of a movable spoiler, like those employed by the Chaparrals, is possible if no other remedy is discovered.

CHARLOTTE MOTOR SPEEDWAY

While Daytona's 2½-mile layout was under construction the idea of building a third superspeedway apparently occurred to two men at the same time—Curtis Turner, widely known for his bullish race driving, and Bruton Smith, a Charlotte real estate broker and part-time promoter.

For more than a year one proposed to build a track south of Charlotte in the heart of the populous Piedmont crescent of the Carolinas. The other favored locating his track north of the Carolinas' largest city, and Charlotte was faced with the prospect of Siamese-twin race tracks, each drawing the life's blood from the other. Finally the race driver and the promoter reached a compromise, combining their efforts to build a single track about 12 miles north of Charlotte.

The First Race

The track was considered an engineering marvel, since it was completed in less than half the time predicted by construction engineers. Unfortunately, however, the surface of the D-shaped track began to break up under the pressure of 60 cars going full bore. It resembled a ploughed field by the time the first race was over.

Curtis Turner and Bruton Smith,
co-founders of Charlotte Motor Speedway.

Cale Yarborough set a new four-lap qualifying record of 154.385 mph to win the pole position for the 1967 World 600.

A relative unknown garnered all the honors in the first race, held on June 19, 1960. Joe Lee Johnson dodged his way to glory by avoiding chunks of flying asphalt as the freshly paved track cracked and peeled. The Tennessee driver averaged 107.752 miles an hour as one favorite after another fell victim to the uncured track surface. Joe Lee started in twentieth position and finished first to take home more than $20,000 for his afternoon's work. More than 50,000 excited race fans had witnessed this first race.

Track Layout

The 1½-mile track is situated on a 554-acre tract on U.S. 29, 12 miles north of Charlotte. The turns are banked 24 degrees with a 5-degree slope on the front- and backstretches. The front straight is interrupted by two slight turns, giving the track a D-shape. The track is 45 feet wide on the straights and 60 feet wide in the turns.

A double strand of 12-inch high, 10-gauge steel guard rail stands between the hurtling cars and a flight into the parking lot as they zip around the asphalt oval at speeds approaching 150 miles an hour. The guard rail is mounted on 10-inch diameter posts set 6 to 8 feet apart. Providing protection to the fans are concrete retaining walls topped off with a 12-foot fence to keep loose wheels out of the stands.

Cale Yarborough holds the current qualifying record at CMS

with a speed of 162.162 miles an hour driving a Ford. The mark was established October 12, 1969.

Originally Charlotte promoted a 600-mile event in the spring (usually the last week in May) and what was a season-ending 400-miler. In 1966 the October race was lengthened to 500 miles and with the addition of a ninth superspeedway the last race of the season is now held at Bryan, Texas, on the first Sunday in December. There are seats for 50,000 fans on the front and back straights with accommodations for at least another 50,000 in the infield.

Races and Personalities

For Fred Lorenzen just the mention of Charlotte Motor Speedway has been like money in the bank, but the Elmhurst, Illinois, driver is having to share the dollar spotlight with Bobby and Donnie Allison. Fred owns four wins, two in the World 600 and two in the National 500 with more than $110,000 in official prize money.

Donnie Allison is right up there in earnings with more than

Charlotte's big winner Fred Lorenzen throws an artificial rose from the winner's circle.

$110,000 and two victories. Donnie has finished in the top five in six of the 10 events he has entered.

Bobby Allison has won over $90,000 at Charlotte with wins in the 1971 World 600 and 1971 National 500 to push his earnings close to the $100,000 mark. Lee Roy Yarbrough has won three times and Jim Paschal, Buddy Baker and Junior Johnson have two victories each.

One of Lorenzen's most exciting wins came in the 1965 National 400 when during the last 50 laps he battled for the lead with A. J. Foyt and Dick Hutcherson bumper-to-bumper and side-by-side down the straights and through the turns.

Only a few miles from the most exciting finish of any race ever staged at Charlotte, the Fords of Lorenzen and Foyt touched in the third turn. Foyt lost control and spun out in the fourth turn. Hutcherson had all he could handle to miss Foyt's spinning car. Curtis Turner, who was in the same lap and only a few car lengths behind, slowed to avoid a collision and lost any chance of catching the flying Lorenzen, who went on to win.

But 1965 wasn't the only year that saw exciting finishes in the double-barrelled events. Junior Johnson, Lorenzen and David Pearson have all shared in the heartbreak of the all-out competition of the National 400, which consistently provided the most exciting finish to the NASCAR season.

Perhaps one of the most frustrating stories is that of Richard Petty, who managed to keep his 1961 Plymouth in contention all the way despite being several miles an hour slower than the "hot dogs." He had outlasted dame fortune to find himself in the same lap with Joe Weatherly's Pontiac, but almost 30 seconds behind. With less than 20 laps to go and Weatherly increasing his lead on each lap, the caution flag came out, and suddenly Petty was almost on Joe's bumper. When the green flag dropped the high-finned Plymouth nearly pushed Weatherly's Pontiac out of the turn, but the big Indian ran away in the straights.

And so it went. Weatherly would pull away by six- to eight-car lengths in the straights, and Petty's superbly handling Plymouth would make up the difference in the turns. It was a valiant try, but the underpowered Plymouth just couldn't muster enough speed to pass the "Clown Prince of Racing," and Petty had to settle for second.

For Junior Johnson, heartbreak came in the form of an empty gas tank in the 1963 World 600 as he pushed his independently sponsored 1963 Chevy to the front and held it there. With three laps remaining, Johnson's engine sputtered and died, allowing Loren-

Ford's brightest hopes for victory in the 1970 National 500 went out when David Pearson lost control, spun and backed into the guard rail and Cale Yarborough (21), who was too close to avoid him, became involved.

zen to grab the lead and the win just when everyone was sure that Johnson's Ray Fox-built Chevy had shown the factory-sponsored cars its bumper.

Lorenzen had the favor returned by Johnson in the 1963 National 400 when it appeared that Lorenzen would be the first driver to win both races in a single year. Lorenzen's car coughed and sputtered, and Johnson rode into victory circle.

Fireball Roberts

It was June 2, 1964, and the skies were a brilliant blue. It was a day destined to haunt the memories of every race fan who attended and also of those who had stayed away. Fireball Roberts had the pole position again, and the Fireball's staunchest rooters said this was the day.

Of the seven races run at Charlotte up to 1963, Fireball had held the pole position five times but had only managed two seconds. This, his fans believed, would be the day he broke the jinx and put his purple Holman-Moody Ford in the winner's circle.

On the seventh lap, it happened. Coming out of the second turn Fireball, Ned Jarrett and Junior Johnson tangled. A huge column of black smoke rose from the blackened hulk of the car which bore No. 22. A hush fell over the stands. Ned Jarrett leaped from his flaming car and ran to aid Fireball. Ned pulled him from the inferno and helped beat out the flames licking at Fireball's driving suit.

Roberts, who had captivated virtually every fan who saw him run with his foot-in-the-carburetor style of driving, hung tenaciously to life for five weeks in a Charlotte hospital. Just when it appeared he might survive his extensive burns, infection set in and death claimed one of the greatest drivers the sport has ever seen.

Driving the Track

For those who sit in the stands it looks simple. For those who must do it, it involves knowing every inch of the asphalt ribbon. A driver studies every bump in the track, knowing that a minute misjudgment could be the last when hurtling along in heavy traffic at better than 145 miles an hour.

Each track has its own characteristics, and there is always one best way around. The fastest way around Charlotte, according to most drivers, is down the front straight as close as possible to the grassy area separating the track from the pit road in the bends of the D and near the middle of the start-finish line.

At the first turn the right door almost brushes the wall before

---

Gordon Johncock jumps into the infield after going high in turn four, smacking the rail and coasting down to hit the inside rail just before the entrance to pit road at Atlanta International Raceway.

the car starts into the high-banked turn. A middle course through the first and second turns leads the car out and into the backstretch near the retaining wall again and then down the back straight just a few feet from the concrete. The third turn brings the car away from the wall and into a high or low groove, depending on the driver's preference. Then it's full throttle as the car goes into the fourth turn and starts out into the homestretch.

One of the most exciting seats at Charlotte is in the fourth turn, where it seems that the cars must slow down or slam into the concrete as they prepare for the long run down the homestretch and the two bends between turn four and the first one.

Qualifying speeds have climbed from the then-respectable 134.429 turned in by Roberts in 1960 to Yarborough's unequaled record of 162.162 miles an hour in 1969.

ATLANTA INTERNATIONAL RACEWAY

It was back in 1959 when Atlanta, Georgia, made its first move toward capturing a share of the national sports spotlight with construction of the 1½-mile Atlanta International Raceway. Thirty thousand tons of asphalt, 120,000 cubic yards of concrete, two miles of guard rail and another four miles of fence went into Georgia's first and only superspeedway, located 20 miles south of Atlanta on U.S. 41. More than $2 million also went into the facility, which allows race cars to travel around the 24-degree banked turns at speeds approaching 160 miles an hour.

Grandstands along either straightaway accommodate 40,000

Cale Yarborough scored his first superspeedway victory in the 1967 Atlanta 500.

people and the 68-acre infield will hold at least that many more. The track has the distinction of having attracted the largest one-day crowd ever to attend a sporting event in Georgia. And this despite stiff competition from such outstanding events as the Masters Golf Tournament at Augusta and more recently the advent of the Atlanta Braves baseball team and the Atlanta Falcons professional football team. The Atlanta 500 race in 1965 drew more than 70,000 people to the track, while the Braves, who were making their debut in Atlanta, managed to draw 14,000.

Atlanta's opening followed Daytona's by two years and lacked only a month of beating Charlotte's superspeedway into operation. It was the fourth supertrack on the NASCAR circuit and helped put Atlanta on the map as a big-time sports center.

Track Layout

The 1½-mile plant is located on a 502-acre site. It lies in the middle of a natural depression which provides excellent viewing from both the grandstands and the infield. The turns are banked 24 degrees and there is a slight bank on the straights. Both the back and front straights measure 1,580 feet in length and are 40 feet wide, opening to 65 feet in the 2,780-foot turns.

Pit road matches the length of the front straight and is 49 feet wide. Pit crews are protected from the hurtling machinery by a two-tiered guard rail next to the track and a concrete wall between pit road and the pits. A field hospital, traffic-light systems in the turns, fire and rescue equipment stationed around the track and a double-tiered steel guard rail around the outside of the track contribute to the safety of the drivers.

Atlanta hosts four major events each year, two for stock cars, one for Indianapolis-type cars and one for Modified-Sportsman cars. The Atlanta 500 is usually scheduled for the first Sunday in April. The Grand National cars return to peach country early in August. In June the Indianapolis drivers invade the high banks of AIR with their low-slung bathtubs on wheels to show southern folk how racing ought to be. Finally, Atlanta is host to the season-ending Modified-Sportsman championship race which can, and has, decided the national point championship.

Three special awards are presented at the Atlanta 500 each year. A diamond victory ring goes to the winning driver. The Paul McDuffie Memorial Trophy goes to the chief mechanic of the winning car, and the Joe Weatherly Memorial Trophy is presented to the most popular driver, selected by a vote of the fans.

Past Winners

Sixteen drivers have shared victory honors since the gates opened at Atlanta. Five drivers have monopolized victory circle with more than one victory.

Fred Lorenzen is tops with four wins. Lorenzen won the Atlanta 500 in 1962, 1963 and 1964. He also won a special 250-mile event in 1961. Cale Yarborough and Richard Petty both claim three victories each. Lee Roy Yarbrough and Marvin Panch have both won twice.

Other winners at Atlanta include A. J. Foyt, David Pearson, Bobby Allison, Bobby Johns, Bob Burdick, Rex White, Junior Johnson, Ned Jarrett, Jim Hurtubise, Dick Hutcherson and Fireball Roberts.

Buddy Baker holds the qualifying record at Atlanta with a time of 164.226 miles an hour set in qualifying for the Atlanta 500 in 1969. Richard Petty drove the fastest race ever staged here in 1970, pushing his 1970 Plymouth to an average speed of 142.712 miles an hour.

Driving the Track

Most tracks have special grooves for high-speed cars. The uniform construction of the Atlanta track makes the fastest route almost a matter of choice to the driver. The track is wide enough for three-abreast competition in the straights and turns, although it is seldom that three cars will run side by side in the turns. There is plenty of room for two fast cars to pass slower traffic in the turns.

Richard Petty likes the high road, and Junior Johnson usually preferred to run low. The majority of the "hot dogs" like the middle groove, straddling the second white line in the turns with the left wheels. Using the middle groove, the cars come out of the turns wide, right next to the concrete retaining walls at the grandstands. As the drivers set up to go into the first and third turns, they move out a few feet.

Atlanta has earned the reputation for close finishes in the past few years. With one or two exceptions, both the Atlanta 500 and Dixie 500 have ended with two or three cars battling for the checkered flag.

Hercules Rides Again

Jim "Hercules" Hurtubise is a small man who has been racing for more than 15 years. He hails from North Tonawanda, New York, but he feels more at home when he is strapped in a race car. Hurtu-

Most drivers prefer to run the middle groove as shown here by Dick Hutcherson (29) and Fred Lorenzen (28) with A. J. Foyt on the inside.

bise is the only USAC driver to invade Georgia and capture a major stock car race. When he took the Atlanta 500 in 1966, the win was almost as devastating as Sherman's march to the sea.

In a near fatal accident in Milwaukee, Wisconsin, in 1964 Hurtubise suffered burns over his face, hands and most of the remainder of his body when his Indy Roadster slammed into the wall after hitting debris in the fourth turn. Very few gave him a chance to recover, much less race again.

But those who doubted hadn't counted on Hurtubise's determination. It was necessary to operate on his hands, and when the doctors asked whether he preferred his fingers locked straight or curved, Herk chose the curved position so he could have a better grasp on the steering wheel of his race car.

Come back he did. He finished third in the 1965 Yankee 300 at Indianapolis. Tire problems kayoed the five-foot, eight-inch bundle of nerves at Daytona in 1966. Then there was Atlanta. Hurtubise could qualify no better than fifth, while Richard Petty's Plymouth was honking at 147-plus. The Petty blue started on the pole and held the front spot for more than 100 miles before lack of oil pressure burned out his engine. Bobby Isaac hit the wall in the fourth turn. The fuel pump on Dave Pearson's Dodge broke in half. Marvin Panch, Curtis Turner and Lee Roy Yarbrough also blew engines.

133

Jim Hurtubise

Hurtubise said his car was vibrating at the start of the race. "I found it vibrated just about the same, whether I ran hard or easy, so I decided to run until something happened," he said later.

When the checkered bunting waved in the breeze, Hurtubise had a full lap lead on the field and was still running strong. Fred Lorenzen summed up the feelings of most NASCAR drivers when he said, "Hurtubise deserved to win. He never shut that Plymouth down."

NORTH CAROLINA MOTOR SPEEDWAY

North Carolina Motor Speedway is nestled in the sandhills about halfway between Rockingham and Hamlet on U.S. 1. The one-mile superspeedway holds one unique distinction. The track had been paid for from the day the first race was run, and not one single monetary problem has bothered the management of the modern racing plant.

It took more than four years to bring the South's first high-speed one-mile track from idea to actuality, but when it was completed it was evident that nothing had been spared to make it a first-class operation. In December of 1964 the track was 15 per cent finished, and designer Harold Brasington of Darlington, South Carolina, found himself without the funds to go on.

Brasington was one of the designers of the Darlington track and a man who believes in creating a challenge for the driver as well as an exciting show for the spectator. The one-mile layout was designed with a low groove in mind, to keep the driver on his toes every minute. There is no chance to rest and let the car and the banked turns do the work.

Brasington turned to a group of local investors for aid in completing the track. J. Elsie Webb, a local attorney, headed the group which consisted of Dr. George Galloway, L. G. DeWitt, L. V. Hogan, Sheriff Raymond Goodman, Hugh Lee, North Lewis, Hubert Lathan, J. M. Long and Bill Land.

Many said a million-dollar racing plant could not survive in such a rural setting in the heart of North Carolina's peach country, but Webb convinced them otherwise. With only a portion of the grading and a handful of concrete grandstands to show for his work, Brasington explained his ideas to the local investors, and their combined efforts produced a finished racing plant in less than a year.

The First Race

In late August of 1965 the last of the paving was completed, and tire firms began testing programs. The first race was scheduled for October 31, 1965. Many doubted that it could be a successful race because of the withdrawal of Chrysler from racing in a dispute with NASCAR over the use of the hemispherical head race engine, and without the MoPar products competing it didn't look good.

With the end of the summer came Chrysler's announcement that it would resume competition on all tracks of one mile or less for the rest of the season. This meant that North Carolina Motor Speedway could count on a full house both in terms of spectators and competitors. The rush was on for tickets to the newest race track's first event, and sales exceeded everyone's wildest dreams.

Race day dawned clear and cold. All roads throughout North and South Carolina led to NCMS that day, and almost 40,000 fans jammed the grandstands and infield to watch the impending battle between Ford and MoPar. The race was billed as a real showdown between such Chrysler greats as Richard Petty, David Pearson *et al* and Ford's Fred Lorenzen, Junior Johnson, Marvin Panch, Dick Hutcherson and last, but by no means least, the old pro himself, Curtis "Pops" Turner.

What Chrysler fans had thought would be their chance to tell everyone what they had been missing all year turned out to be a Ford runaway with a driver who had competed in only two NASCAR events in four years doing the honors.

Despite several cracked ribs suffered in a race two weeks be-

Junior Johnson (26) leads Richard Petty (43) into the first turn during the inaugural American 500 in 1965.

fore, "Pops" Turner as he has become affectionately known, drove his Wood Brothers-prepared 1965 Ford to a convincing win ahead of teammate Cale Yarborough. It was a personal victory for Turner and a further triumph for Ford in a season full of wins.

There was some doubt whether Curtis' reflexes were up to par, but fans didn't have to wait long to find out that his foot was just as heavy as it had been before his departure four years earlier.

In the National 400 at Charlotte, "Leadfoot" had managed a third place finish, and at Rockingham he withstood the challenges offered by Richard Petty, Junior Johnson, Marvin Panch and Bobby Isaac to claim more than $13,000 in first-place prize money.

As he climbed smiling from his racer in victory circle, it required great effort for the forty-two-year-old driver just to talk, but he didn't have to say a word. The cheers were deafening and must have been music to his weary ears.

Driving the Track

The drivers seem to agree that North Carolina Motor Speedway is in a class with Darlington when it comes to getting around the low-groove track. The turns are banked, but not steeply enough to allow going through full bore. Just as at Darlington, each driver seems to have his own secret for finding his way around the fast course. The real trick is negotiating the first and third turns, and the solution seems to lie in bringing the car down from a position next to the retaining wall.

In the first turn the transition from flat-out to cornering comes about 100 feet from the start of the turn as the cars seem almost to jerk to the left to set up for the turn. The fastest route appears to be just about the middle, bringing the car out low and then back up against the wall which protects fans in the stands along the backstretch.

The process is almost identical in the third turn, with the cars able to ride just a little higher through the third and fourth turns and to come out of No. 4 full bore for the start-finish line. There just isn't much room to pass in the turns, as anyone who has rubbed fenders will testify. Most of the "hot dogs" will bump whoever happens to be in front of them rather than take a chance of losing it in one of these turns.

One of the major problems at NCMS is the sun, which sets between the first and second turns near the end of the race. During the first few tire tests the problem didn't bother anyone, because the tests were conducted during full daylight and the heat of day. However, on the first day of qualifying, those who waited until late in the afternoon to take advantage of a cooling track for better traction found themselves blinded as they entered the first turn and couldn't see a thing until they started out of the second turn. Wide strips of tape were pasted across the top of the windshield to add a little protection from the sun, and the drivers by shifting position in the seat managed to get through without any real mishaps.

In the first turn Curtis Turner (13) blows his engine, spins out and forces Dick Hutcherson into the guard rail.

Richard Petty (43) and Fred Lorenzen (28) exchanged the lead officially 11 times during the first 290 miles of the 1966 American 500.

Schedule of Events

A shift in dates for the first race of the year at NCMS from March to June could eliminate the sun problem for one of the two annual 500-milers.

In 1966 the spring race was run in March and known as the Peach Blossom 500 because the race came at the height of the peach orchard's beauty. In 1967 the spring event was rescheduled for mid-June and renamed the Carolina 500, since the speedway is located near the heart of both Carolinas. In 1968 it was moved back to March due to scheduling problems and is still held during the first or second week in March.

The second event, the American 500, has proved to be one of the most exciting races on the circuit, with Ford receiving most of the benefits so far.

In 1965 Turner and Ford proved that Chrysler wasn't all that hot, and nobody, least of all the Ford drivers, missed them after all. In 1966 it was Ford's turn to stand idle in a dispute with NASCAR over the use of the single overhead cam engine.

Ford also came back and with a vengeance, switching from the Category I Galaxie to the Category II Fairlane. Lorenzen drove

138

a Fairlane at Darlington and finished respectably. At Martinsville he won in this smaller, lighter and more economical car.

At NCMS in the American 500 there was a tremendous battle between Lorenzen and Richard Petty from the moment the green flag fell, with the two foremost drivers for the opposing factions—Ford vs. Chrysler—doing battle as most racing fans had longed to see all year.

During the first 290 miles of the race Lorenzen and Petty exchanged the lead 11 times officially, but most onlookers lost count of the times the pair traded places within the same lap, which didn't count as official lead changes. Petty lost time on a pit stop at lap 287, and from there on out Lorenzen continued to build up his lead. It appeared for a while that Petty might catch the low-flying Lorenzen, as he pushed his Plymouth to the limit in a vain effort to overtake the Fairlane. Lorenzen set a track record for the 500 miles at 104.348 miles an hour.

Cale Yarborough

Cale Yarborough was determined to make it to victory circle at NCMS, since he already owned two seconds and two fourths there. He finished second to Curtis Turner and Paul Goldsmith in his first two tries and was the only driver within striking distance of Lorenzen in 1966, but the "Lady in Black" caught up with him and ended any chances of catching Lorenzen.

A bump-up during the final stages of the race, as he went into

After hitting the guard rail in the first turn and some fast pit work to get sheet metal off the left rear tire, Cale Yarborough gets back into the action.

J. Elsie Webb, president of the North Carolina Motor Speedway, congratulates Ned Jarrett on winning the trophy which bears his name.

the first turn, sent Yarborough's Ford crashing into the guard rail and from there to the pits to have the sheet metal altered enough to allow him to complete the race.

It wasn't until 1970, when Cale won the American 500 with a record-breaking speed of 119.811 mph, that he was able to overcome the apparent jinx that this track held for him.

Ned Jarrett Trophy

When NCMS officials learned that the 1966 American 500 was to be Ned Jarrett's last race in a career which spanned seven years on the Grand National circuit, they decided to award a trophy each year to the person who contributed most to the rookie drivers on the circuit. Jarrett's willingness to act as racing's goodwill ambassador helped bring stock car racing from the doldrums of just another sport to the recognition many have long sought for it.

The Newton-Conover, North Carolina, native won the NAS-CAR Sportsman championships in 1957 and 1958. He went on to capture the Grand National point championship in 1961 and again in 1965. Jarrett won 50 Grand National races during those seven years and claimed more than $250,000 in prize money for his efforts, but he was never too busy to speak before any group wanting to know about racing. The trophy which bears his name is awarded by a secret ballot of the rookie drivers. The first recipient—Ned Jarrett himself.

Improvements

North Carolina Motor Speedway was one of the most modern racing plants in the country the day its gates first opened to the public, and efforts to stay No. 1 have been continued, with more and bigger changes promised for the future. The bare infield now has a carpet of lush grass. A new airstrip has been built 200 yards from the grandstands for the convenience of those who prefer to fly in. The most modern concessions and rest rooms have been installed along with a completely air-conditioned press box and facilities equal to those at most major football stadiums.

In 1969 the turns were rebuilt with the banking increased and a new tunnel leading into the infield was added under the fourth turn.

The change in the degree of banking in the turns resulted in a major increase in qualifying speeds. Cale Yarborough held the old record of 118.717 miles an hour set in 1968. With the higher banks, Bobby Allison holds the current record of 139.048 miles an hour set in 1970 qualifying for the Carolina 500.

141

One fan leaving the speedway after a recent race was over-heard commenting that the one thing he liked more than anything else was the fact that he could see every foot of the race track from his seat.

ALABAMA INTERNATIONAL MOTOR SPEEDWAY

Alabama International Motor Speedway is the newest of the southern circuit superspeedways. Located at Talladega, Alabama, about 45 miles from Birmingham, the 2.66-mile paved high bank track holds the distinction of being the fastest of the super tracks.

Construction of the facility began in 1967 on a 1,000-acre site which includes part of an airport facility at Talladega. The track is located just off Interstate 20 within easy driving range of Georgia, Tennessee, Alabama and Mississippi and portions of North and South Carolina, Florida, Kentucky and Arkansas.

Bill France, president of NASCAR and promoter of the facility, estimates population within driving distance of the track between 15 and 20 million.

Talladega has failed to live up to early predictions of drawing larger crowds than Daytona (about 100,000 since 1967), but part of the blame lies with uncomplete interstate roads (scheduled for completion in early 1972).

The track has been described as a "quad oval" with bowed front and back stretches. The high-banked turns allow competing cars to run "flat out" all the way around the track.

Talladega hosts two 500-mile events—the Alabama 500 in May and the Talladega 500 in August—for stock cars. The track is also the scene of motorcycle races, sports car events and Grand American and Modified-Sportsman races.

First Race

The first race resulted in one of the biggest controversies in the history of NASCAR. More than 20 of the top drivers refused to race on the newly paved surface because tires were shredding to pieces at racing speeds.

Charlie Glotzbach set the qualifying mark of 199.466 miles an hour in a Dodge built by Ray Nichels and sponsored by Dow Chemical Co. Tires were shredding a strip about two inches wide in the center of the tire after only five or six laps at racing speeds of about 195 miles an hour.

Special tires were flown in after qualifying, but they continued to shred. The Professional Drivers Association met with Bill France and asked that the race be postponed until the track seasoned and tires could be developed to withstand the tremendous speeds.

The drivers had complained about rough conditions in the first turn and a washboard effect at several other points on the track. France asked that the drivers hold their speeds to 185 miles an hour or less to keep from shredding tires.

Most of the top drivers refused to race on the track surface as it was, because they said it was too dangerous.

France decided to go ahead and stage the race anyway, because the drivers didn't leave until the day before the race. The field consisted of a few GN cars which did not leave, Grand American cars which had been on hand for a race the day before and anything else that France could find which resembled a race car.

Richard Brickhouse of Rocky Point, North Carolina was the winner of the inaugural event which was more of a parade than a race. Speeds were held in the 185-mile-an-hour bracket, but even at the reduced speeds Bobby Isaac and others encountered shredding problems.

Brickhouse, driving the car Glotzbach had qualified, averaged only 153.778 miles an hour despite the virtually wreck-free race.

Other Winners

Pete Hamilton is the only driver with two wins at Talladega. The former Sportsman champ took the checkered flag twice while driving the second Petty Plymouth.

Donnie Allison and brother Bobby also own victories at the world's fastest closed circuit track. Pete Hamilton holds the race record of 158.517 miles an hour set in August of 1970 while Bobby Isaac owns the qualifying mark of 199.658 miles an hour set in April of 1970.

Donnie Allison's win in May of 1970 stands out as the most exciting race in the brief history of the track.

Four cars staged a trophy dash race which lasted for 490 miles and then three battled it out for the checkered flag. Donnie drove the Wood Brothers Mercury while brother Bobby was behind the wheel of the Holman-Moody Ford, Buddy Baker wheeled the Petty Dodge entry and Dave Marcis was driving the K&K Insurance Dodge after Bobby Isaac suffered an attack of gallstones.

The four drivers swapped the lead throughout the event with Marcis hanging back at first and then challenging the more experienced "hot dogs."

The final 50 laps saw the cars closely bunched and exchanging the lead several times on each lap. With less than 10 laps remaining, Marcis made his bid, but as he crossed the start/finish line with seven laps to go, the engine came apart.

The Allison brothers and Baker battled those last few laps with Donnie finishing first and Bobby just nosing out Baker's Dodge for second.

World's Records

Bobby Isaac not only owns the fastest qualifying speed for a closed course of 2.66 miles, but also is the holder of the record speed of 201.104 set in November of 1970.

Buddy Baker is the only other driver to have averaged in excess of 200 miles an hour, a record he set in 1969.

Isaac's qualifying record of 199.658 miles an hour is expected to hold up for some time due to the restrictive sleeves which have been imposed on carburetors and have slowed the cars down about 10 to 15 miles an hour.

Other Superspeedways Contemplated

Superspeedways at Ontario, California and Pocono International Speedway in Long Pond, Pennsylvania, have hosted NASCAR Grand National events. Both tracks are 2.5 miles in length and incorporate the most modern facilities.

Plans are in the works for several other tracks of at least one mile in length with rumors locating one near Richmond, Virginia and another near Raleigh, North Carolina.

Race tracks at Irish Hills, Michigan and College Station, Texas have gone into operation with two events scheduled each year. Both tracks are two miles in length and boast speeds between 160 and 170 miles an hour.

Both tracks have experienced financial and managerial problems which appear to have been straightened out at this point. Michigan has held races since 1969, and the Bryan facility has recently come under new management which has set up a schedule of racing.

144

9

THE SMALLER PAVED TRACKS

BRISTOL INTERNATIONAL SPEEDWAY

A soft wind carries the roar of straining metal across the hills of Virginia and Tennessee as the closely bunched pack of race cars whizzes around the 24-degree banked turns of the half-mile Bristol International Speedway. Built in 1961 at a cost of more than $1 million, Bristol has become one of the most popular sites for Grand National races as well as a mecca for drag racing in the East.

The hollow sound of exhaust beating against the concrete stands, which accommodate more than 25,000 race fans, can escape only in the turns because the track lies between two ridges. Located just inside Tennessee at Bristol, which is split right down the main street by the Tennessee-Virginia state line, the track hosts a pair of 250-mile Grand National events each year.

A special $100,000 lighting system makes weekly Modified and Late Model Sportsman events possible. In 1964 Bristol added a NHRA-sanctioned drag strip and hosts the Spring Nationals each June. The Southeastern 500 is held in March and the Volunteer 500 in July. Seldom is the winner of either race decided until the final few laps.

Fred Lorenzen has been in victory circle three times at Bristol. His toughest race was the 1964 Volunteer 500 when he and Richard Petty battled for the lion's share of a purse in excess of $20,000. Ned

Jarrett had to relieve Lorenzen during one segment of the race, after injuries Lorenzen had suffered earlier in the month at Daytona started bothering him. Lorenzen watched from the pits as Jarrett dogged Petty but just couldn't coax enough out of Lorenzen's pearl-white Ford to get past him.

On the final pit stop Lorenzen went back into his car for the battle down to the checkered flag. With two laps remaining Petty's lead appeared insurmountable. The margin was almost a full lap and the blue Plymouth showed no signs of slowing down.

And then it happened. As Petty started out of the fourth turn to take the white flag, signifying one lap remaining, smoke boiled out from under the Plymouth, and Petty had to coast. Lorenzen caught him in the third turn and took his third victory at Bristol with a record speed of 78.044 miles an hour.

Donnie Allison holds the current record for the 250-mile distance of 87.543 miles an hour set in the 1970 Southeastern 500. Cale Yarborough holds the qualifying mark of 107.375 miles an hour set in July of 1970.

A field of 36 cars blasts off at Bristol International Speedway.

The going can get crowded on Bristol's half-mile oval. Here Jimmy Helms (58) and Buck Baker (88) move over to let Dick Hutcherson (29) and David Pearson (6) go by in the second turn.

Action is plentiful at the picturesque track, with the hairiest moments coming during the crowded scramble to get through the turns. Although pretty well banked, the approaches to the turns are almost flat, making things difficult at best. One of the most spectacular smashups was during the 1966 Southeastern 500 when Bobby Isaac, driving Junior Johnson's Ford, ripped up almost a dozen iron guard rail posts in the first turn after having problems with the front end.

The Bristol track was rebuilt in 1969, raising the elevation of the banked turns and banking both the front and back straights. The major changes resulted in qualifying speeds increasing almost 20 miles an hour and average race speeds jumping about 10 miles an hour.

The grind of 500 laps over the half-mile track is demanding. In that same event Dick Hutcherson took the checkered flag after David Pearson, Fred Lorenzen, Marvin Panch, Jim Paschal, Cale Yarborough, Ned Jarrett and Paul Goldsmith fell by the wayside with mechanical troubles. Hutcherson was driving the only factory-backed car to finish the race. His car hadn't been the fastest, but it turned out to be the strongest, and that's what counts when you back up to the pay window.

MARTINSVILLE SPEEDWAY

Martinsville Speedway dates back to 1947 when H. Clay Earles, Sam Rice and Henry Lawrence staged the first race over the half-mile dirt layout. Twenty years later, an old-time visitor would not believe his eyes. The red clay oval has a new coat of asphalt, stands which will accommodate 21,000 fans and boxwoods in the turns.

The first race was a financial success, but a disaster for many of the spectators who came straight from church to the race track in their Sunday finest.

"None of us knew much about racing back then," Earles recalls. "We had some fill dirt around the edges of the track, and some of the ladies who wore high heels sank down to their ankles."

More than 6,000 fans paid to see Red Byron capture the first race. From this initial event the Martinsville, Virginia, track has grown to the point where four major events are staged each year with the Grand National and Modified Divisions sharing the spotlight.

Located just south of Martinsville on U.S. 220, the speedway hosts the Virginia 500 in the spring and the Old Dominion 500 in the fall. Both are 500-lap, 250-mile events for Grand National cars. In 1966 Martinsville added a 300-lap Modified-Sportsman event in October and another in the spring of 1967. On the day preceding each of the Grand National races the track holds a special 100-lap Modified-Sportsman event.

Richard Petty (43) finds he has plenty of company in the virtually flat turns at Martinsville.

One of the last races run on dirt at Martinsville Speedway in 1955 shows the cloud of dust which brought about the paving of the track.

Until September of 1962 Ford had never won at Martinsville. But with Nelson Stacey's win in the Old Dominion 500, Ford began a domination of Martinsville which has been broken only twice—in 1966 when Jim Paschal pushed his Plymouth across the finish line first and in 1967 when Richard Petty won the Virginia 500 in his Plymouth.

Fred Lorenzen had dominated the eight races since 1963 with five wins, four of which came in a row starting in 1963 and running through 1965. Lorenzen was appearing in the winner's circle so often that many suggested changing the name of the track to Lorenzen Speedway.

In 1966 Lorenzen made his debut in a Ford Fairlane at the Southern 500 at Darlington, and his second outing in the Category II car was at Martinsville.

It was a ding-dong battle with Ned Jarrett in front at the end of 100 miles. Then Bobby Allison, driving a year-old Chevelle which had been considered underpowered (using a 350 CID engine), grabbed the lead and staved off all challengers for the next 100 miles. His engine finally gave out with less than 50 miles remaining, and Lorenzen put his Holman-Moody Fairlane out front and stayed there all the way. But this was not the end. A protest was filed, charging that Lorenzen's car had an oversized fuel tank. After technical inspectors finished tearing down the top five cars, Lorenzen's and each of the other top finishers' cars were ruled legal.

David Pearson holds the qualifying record with a speed of 87.358 miles an hour set in September of 1969. Richard Petty owns the race record set in the 1970 rain-delayed Old Dominion 500 of 72.159 miles an hour. Petty has more than a half dozen victories to his credit here.

Two names dominate the Modified-Sportsman events—Perk Brown and Ray Hendrick. In the 15 events held at Martinsville since 1960 the pair have collected nine wins.

NORTH WILKESBORO SPEEDWAY

The location of the ⅝-mile North Wilkesboro Speedway in the foothills of the Blue Ridge Mountains is considered appropriate, since the sport of stock car racing derives at least a portion of its avid interest from the wild tales of bootleggers running from the revenuers in souped-up cars. The single-groove track with a seating capacity of just over 9,000 has a justly deserved reputation as the fastest short track on the NASCAR circuit.

Bobby Isaac holds the qualifying mark established in April of 1970 with a speed of 107.040 miles an hour. Bobby Allison holds the record for the fastest 250-mile event with a speed of 95.268 set in 1969 in the Mario Ross Dodge.

The late Fireball Roberts and the North Wilkesboro Speedway went into the racing business on the same date, May 16, 1947. The track was originally a dirt oval. In 1959 the track was paved and in 1961 the two major NASCAR races were inaugurated. The Gwyn Staley Memorial race is run each spring and the Wilkes 250 is held each fall. The original 2,400 seating accommodations were expanded to 9,000 when the track was paved. The popular speedway usually attracts around 15,000 to each of the major races.

Competition is keen on this slick track which allows safe passing only in the straights, since both turns are single-groove curves. Jim Paschal effectively blocked Richard Petty for more than 50 laps during the 1966 Gwyn Staley event and went on to win after Petty blew.

The two had things pretty much to themselves during the race after Paul Goldsmith and Sam McQuagg lost oil filters and sprayed engine parts all over the track. Previously Ford had withdrawn from racing in a dispute over the single overhead cam engine. With 60 laps remaining, the battle was furious. Petty had a few car lengths lead on Paschal when the telltale puff of smoke appeared under Petty's car sending him behind the pit wall and out of the race.

North Wilkesboro seems to have Paschal's number. He won in the spring event, but the fall of 1966 will be one that the High Point, North Carolina, driver may never forget.

It was during practice the day before the race, and two women who had been watching practice runs from the infield decided to leave. They got into their car and started across the track to head for the exit. Paschal, among others, was still practicing, and his red Plymouth barreled down the straight. He swerved to avoid the intruding car, but to no avail, and smashed into the women's car. As a result of the impact the entire right side of his car was ripped open but fortunately no one was seriously injured.

Paschal's crew chief, Bill Ellis, worked all night to ready the car which started in 35th position. Paschal drove his way up, finishing fourth. His accident will probably be remembered much longer than Tom Pistone's mishap on the sixth lap of that race or even the grinding crash which demolished Darel Dieringer's Mercury Comet. There's never a dull moment at North Wilkesboro Speedway.

The cars get the green flag at Asheville-Weaverville Speedway.

ASHEVILLE-WEAVERVILLE SPEEDWAY

The world's fastest half-mile stock car track was built by a road contractor on his own property while his grading equipment was idle. Gene Sluder of Weaverville, North Carolina, puttered around in his back lot for a couple of years, and suddenly he had himself a swift, well-banked, half-mile oval.

Located about 10 miles north of Asheville in the heart of the Blue Ridge Mountains of North Carolina, Asheville-Weaverville Speedway sits in a small valley with grandstands on either side and good seats high above the first and second turns. Paved in 1958, the track quickly earned the reputation of being as fast as greased lightning.

Cotton Owens remembers that first race. "I ought to remember it all right," the car builder says. "I went into the first turn too hard. About halfway through everything broke loose, and I crunched the wall in the second turn."

Asheville-Weaverville has been the scene of nine western North Carolina 500 races since the track was paved, and there have been nine different winners, including Richard Petty and Darel Dieringer. A new race was added in 1965, the Fireball 300, a 150-mile event named after the famed Fireball Roberts. From 10-lap dashes to a grueling, 250-mile test of men and machinery, Asheville-Weaverville packs them in with a good view of all the action.

And usually there's plenty of action. Asheville-Weaverville isn't a wide track at best, and with speeds approaching 90 miles an hour on a track full of race cars, things can get pretty hairy in a hurry.

Bobby Allison owns the track qualifying record with a speed of 90.407 miles an hour set in 1967. Fred Lorenzen's 1963 pace of 77.67 miles an hour still stands for a 250-mile event but Marvin Panch averaged 81.669 miles an hour in a 100-mile event in 1964 and Petty holds the record for a 150-mile event with an average speed of 83.36 miles an hour, set in 1967.

There's one race at Asheville-Weaverville that will never be forgotten. The spring snows had melted with an early thaw, and then a hard freeze hit the mountains of western North Carolina and eastern Tennessee. A full field of NASCAR Grand National cars invaded the quiet hills with their staccato exhaust. The melted snow had just time to work down into the base under the pavement when the sharp drop in temperature froze the base, causing it to expand. Before the 4,000-pound cars had run 100 laps the pavement was coming up in chunks the size of manhole covers.

Little Joe Weatherly took a piece of asphalt about the size of a pie plate through the right side of his windshield. Little Joe told a fellow driver that the chunk of asphalt would have decapitated him had it come in on the other side. NASCAR officials decided to halt the race as soon as it passed the halfway point.

Sluder sold his interest to 12 other promoters including Bill France, Joe Littlejohn, Raymond Parks, Jim Foster and Grafton Burgess in 1966. According to several of the promoters, plans for improving the physical plant were in the works, but the last race held here was in 1969.

LEADING DRIVERS

Nine drivers dominated the short paved tracks during 1964, 1965 and 1966. Two of the top asphalt drivers have hung up their helmets after successful careers, and the rest of the field might well be very glad.

Junior Johnson, a threat on any race track, owned 10 wins in 39 races on paved tracks of a half-mile or less. Ned Jarrett, who earned the GN point championship twice in his career, was close behind with seven firsts. Old Bridge, New Jersey, a ½-mile track; Old Dominion Speedway in Manassas, Virginia, a ⅜-mile layout; the ⅓-mile New Asheville (North Carolina) Speedway and the ¼-mile Bowman Gray Stadium in Winston-Salem, North Carolina, were favorite haunts of Junior Johnson.

Ned Jarrett apparently fell in love with the ³⁄₁₀-mile Harris (North Carolina) Speedway; Moyock Raceway's ⅓-mile layout in Moyock, North Carolina, and the ½-mile Speedway in Beltsville, Maryland, as he dominated the action at these tracks.

Richard Petty and Dick Hutcherson were right behind the two leaders with six wins each over the three years. Half-mile tracks at Nashville, Tennessee; Augusta, Georgia; and Moyock Raceway proved popular with the pair. Hutcherson owns two wins at Moyock, Augusta and Nashville. Petty can claim two at Augusta and three at Nashville. David Pearson and Fred Lorenzen claim many wins at these short tracks too.

A new trend appeared during 1966, as three unfamiliar names began appearing in the win column. Only one of the three was really a new name, as Tiny Lund and Elmo Langley have been around for a long time. But the shocker came with the appearance of a young newcomer.

His name is Bobby Allison, and his experience as Modified champion gave him the idea. Somewhere he found the courage to try something which had drawn nothing more than guffaws when mentioned around the pits. The concept was simple: The less weight you have to push around, the fewer horsepower necessary to do the job. Seeing how successfully the 327 CID Sportsman cars were outrunning the Grand National cars on the short tracks, he decided to sacrifice a few horses for the reduced weight with an accompanying fuel saving. Thus, fewer pit stops.

Maine residents turned out in droves to watch Richard Petty and other famous stock car drivers inaugurate the sport in New England. Much to everyone's surprise that warm July night in Oxford, Bobby Allison brought his year-old Chevelle home first. Four days later he proved it wasn't a fluke by showing his rear bumper to the field at Islip, New York, and then he showed them how to do it at Beltsville, Maryland.

In September, with Ford back in the thick of competiton in the Fairlane and the smaller (396 CID) engine, Allison ran like a scared rabbit at a greyhound track until his 350 CID engine came apart. His comfortable lead over Fred Lorenzen, who went on to win the 250-miler over the ½-mile Martinsville track, melted along with his engine. But the youngster had left his mark.

Bobby Allison has continued his winning ways both on the small tracks and the superspeedways. A fierce competitor, Allison got the Holman-Moody ride in 1971 when Pearson went with Chris Vallo and the Pontiac team. Since joining the H-M team Allison has won

Bobby Allison

Dave Pearson

Tiny Lund

seven superspeedway events and a number of short track events.

Richard Petty, David Pearson, Bobby Isaac, Allison and James Hylton have dominated the short tracks in recent years.

THRILLS OF SMALL TRACKS

The small asphalt tracks come in almost any size. Baton Rouge, Louisiana, and Birmingham, Alabama, are ⅝-mile tracks. Trenton, New Jersey, is a one-mile track. Nashville, Tennessee; Augusta and Macon, Georgia; and Beltsville, Maryland, come in the ½-mile variety. South Boston and Manassas, Virginia, offer ⅜-mile tracks.

Richmond, Virginia; Asheville, North Carolina; Chattanooga, Tennessee; and Oxford, Maine, have ⅓-mile tracks. Randleman and Winston-Salem, North Carolina, have ¼-mile layouts. Islip, New York, boasts a ⅕-mile course while Harris, North Carolina, has a ³⁄₁₀-mile track.

Virtually all the smaller paved ovals started out in life as dirt tracks, but with the ever-increasing trend toward paved facilities for superspeedways, the smaller tracks have followed suit.

Bristol and Beltsville are the only half-mile tracks which were intended to be asphalt when built. Martinsville, North Wilkesboro, Asheville-Weaverville, Nashville and most of the others were converted through the years. Nashville and Islip boast figure-eight tracks as a part of their racing plants. Although not sanctioned by NASCAR, the figure-eight tracks along with demolition derbies have attracted many fans.

The trend away from fairgrounds racing plants has continued over the years, just as horse racing diminished in popularity as an annual fair event. The tracks at Richmond, Nashville, Charlotte (since torn down to make way for a shopping center) and countless others ran horses for years and gradually made the changeover. The same thing has and is happening to the dirt tracks.

The short paved tracks provide more than their share of excitement for the simple reason that there has to be plenty of fender banging. Due to the length and width of the tracks, there just isn't quite enough room to maneuver. Some of them are so short, in fact, that the last car in the field has barely cleared the start-finish line before the green flag falls on the pole-sitter. With confined quarters and fierce competition there are bound to be altercations.

August 27, 1966, is one date that fans at Bowman Gray stadium in Winston-Salem, will never forget. Old pro Curtis Turner, driving a Junior Johnson Ford, and Bobby Allison squared off in a battle which threatened to turn into a riot with a portion of the 15,000 spectators joining in.

Allison had been bumping Turner in the tight turns on the quarter-mile track in an effort to get by the veteran, but had little success. What started out as friendly nudges degenerated into an all-out war. It reached a point where Turner pulled off the track onto the infield and waited for Allison to come around again, whereupon Turner rammed him. Both drivers had to be ejected from the race before peace was restored.

J. T. Putney of Arden, North Carolina, probably still has the lump to prove it, and Tiny Lund has a canceled check to remind him of the punch that cost him $100 and a 30-day probation after an incident at Fonda, New York.

Putney and Lund were involved in a smashup which kayoed five cars on the 14th lap of a 100-miler on July 14, 1966. Putney qualified second and grabbed the early lead. He held it through lap 14 when he went high in the second turn, rode an escape road to the third turn where he tried to pull back onto the track. When he did he was broadside in front of Tiny. Bobby Allison, Elmo Langley and Lyles Stetler went out with the two big men. (Putney stands 6 feet, 2 inches and weighs 215, Tiny is 6 feet, 5 inches and 270 pounds). When both drivers returned to the pits there were some words, and Tiny landed a right cross to Putney's jaw, knocking Putney out. Such incidents make for exciting races, but are soon forgotten by the antagonists.

10

THE DIRT TRACKS

"A little dirt never hurt anyone" is an overworked phrase, but it's a good thing for Grand National drivers who compete and fans who watch to keep in mind at the hard clay ovals where stock car racing got its start.

Drivers and fans alike come out looking several shades redder than when they started. Still there are those drivers and fans who prefer the rough and ready competition of these short bumpy tracks to the smoothest (and far cleaner) superspeedway and the biggest purse ever paid. From out of the cornfields of yesteryear have evolved some highly sophisticated dirt racing plants which consistently attract top drivers and thousands of fans each year.

Not nearly as popular today as they were a dozen years ago, dirt tracks have fallen prey to the paved superspeedway and the small-track promoter who put asphalt over that brick-hard red clay. The transition period began with the completion of Darlington International Raceway in 1950, but it didn't really have drastic effects until a decade later.

By 1955 the trend toward paved tracks was established; red clay gave way grudgingly to the smooth mixture of tar and gravel. Martinsville changed. New superspeedways were built and paved. New short tracks sprang up from Maine to Florida, many of which were paved on opening day. Others followed suit within a few years. During the early years of NASCAR competition, all the races were run on dirt. Even after Darlington went into operation some 90 per cent of the races would have done the dust bowl justice.

But with the completion of Daytona, Charlotte and Atlanta in the early 1960s the trend gathered momentum. In the beginning it was "build a special car for the asphalt tracks." Today the outcry from most drivers and car builders is that the cost of maintaining or making the switch from asphalt to dirt equipment is too expensive for the number of races run. The purse for a 100-mile event is just over $7,000. Of this $1,500 goes to the winner, $800 to the second place man and so on down the line.

Dirt tracks require looser springs and shocks and plenty of extra parts, since those potholes take their toll of equipment. A series of special gears for the various length tracks is necessary in order to be competitive. When the factories footed the bill this was no real problem. But in recent years the factories have been providing support for less than half the races, and those they do support are mainly the long-distance prestige events on paved tracks with high purses.

Because of complaints from spectators—those who don't particularly care for red clay with their hot dogs—and as an accommodation to dirt-covered drivers, the promoters have relented and paved the tracks to keep the fans happy and insure a large field of competitors. In 1965 there were 54 Grand National NASCAR events. Of these 19 were staged on 12 dirt race tracks. In 1966 there were 49 races. Of these 15 were dirt events on 10 tracks. David Pearson won 10 of the 15 races in 1966 driving a two-year-old car. Less than a dozen dirt events were slated for 1967. The last dirt track Grand National race was run in 1970. With the withdrawal of factory support, only one major tire manufacturer participating in racing on the GN level and complaints from the drivers and spectators alike, it was just a matter of time.

SIZES AND RECORDS

The Orange Speedway at Hillsborough, North Carolina, is the longest and fastest dirt track on the NASCAR Grand National circuit. The almost flat 9/10-mile track has a qualifying record of 99.784 miles an hour set in 1964 by David Pearson. The record for a 100-mile event here is 87.25 miles an hour made by Red White in 1962. Ned Jarrett set a record for a 150-mile event in 1965 when he posted an average speed of 90.663 miles an hour.

Perhaps the most popular length of the dirt tracks has been

and will continue to be a half-mile. Virginia State Fairgrounds in Richmond, Virginia; Smoky Mountain Racetrack in Maryville, Tennessee; Greenville-Pickens Speedway in Greenville, South Carolina; Fonda Speedway in Fonda, New York; Columbia Speedway in Columbia, South Carolina; Savannah Speedway, Savannah, Georgia; and Piedmont Interstate Fairgrounds in Spartanburg, South Carolina, as well as Hickory Speedway (⁴⁄₁₀-mile) in Hickory, North Carolina, have done well over the years. Langley Field Speedway in Hampton, Virginia, and Starlite Speedway in Monroe, North Carolina, are ⁴⁄₁₀-mile layouts, with the Virginia track being almost flat while Monroe's turns are well banked.

The tracks are sanctioned by NASCAR, and run weekly events. Twice a year, if the dates are available, the promoters will bring in the Grand Nationals and usually draw an overflow crowd. Fender banging and the spectacular power slides, as the drivers set their cars up for the turns, help bring the dirt-track enthusiasts back year after year.

Many of the drivers who are now competing in the Grand National Division worked their way up through the ranks of Hobby and either the Sportsman or Modified Divisions and are very familiar with the smaller tracks. Junior Johnson and Ned Jarrett both called Hickory home at one time, and both drivers know their way around the hard-packed oval like the backs of their own hands. They collected numerous wins in all divisions at the popular track. David Pearson calls Spartanburg, South Carolina, home and the

Junior Johnson   Ned Jarrett

160

tough competitor owns a half dozen qualifying and race records on half-mile dirt tracks all along the East Coast.

Fonda, New York, has the distinction of holding the fastest qualifying record for half-mile dirt tracks with a speed of 80.801 set by David Pearson in 1968. The Smoky Mountain Raceway in Maryville, Tennessee holds the fastest race record of a 100-mile dirt-track race with a speed of 72.919 miles an hour set in 1967 by Richard Petty.

THE FUTURE

The fans like dirt track events, but the costs of staging these once-common races have soared to the point where the promoter is often forced to pay as much extra money in guarantees to race drivers as he has to put up for the purse.

The pressure for the past decade has been to convert to pavement and the fans have seen the last Grand National event run on dirt. An era of NASCAR racing has come to an end.

The tracks will continue to operate with NASCAR sanctions. However the emphasis will switch to the lighter and faster Modified and Sportsman Divisions. Hobby cars will compete on both dirt and asphalt, but the events will be confined to the shorter tracks. As the number of major tracks increases on the Grand National circuit, the small dirt track promoters will continue to feel the pressure and eventually will be squeezed out.

No one who ever witnessed a Grand National event on dirt can ever forget the powerslides of Curtis Turner, the unique sound of Buck Baker's Chevrolets and Chryslers or the competitive nature of Fireball Roberts, Little Joe Weatherly, Ralph Moody, the Myers brothers or the Flocks.

Virtually every driver has more fun driving on dirt, but it just isn't practical anymore. Bent sheet metal was an indication after a dirt track race that the driver had been in the thick of things. At today's speeds on asphalt there is no room for fender bending to improve position.

Although thousands of fans mourn the loss of dirt track competition, it is a sign that GN racing is growing up. There is still plenty of racing on dirt for Modified and Sportsman cars, both at NASCAR tracks and the outlaw bullrings and dust bowls.

11

THE ROAD COURSES

RIVERSIDE INTERNATIONAL RACEWAY

In late January a 500-mile NASCAR event is held on the tricky nine-turn Riverside International Raceway, marking the first appearance of the new model cars. Built in 1957, Riverside has climbed to the top of internationally known race courses by encompassing every phase of racing and hosting several major events each year. Situated on a 600-acre site just east of Riverside, California, the raceway draws spectators from a population of 7,000,000 people living within 100 miles of the track.

The versatile layout incorporates five different race tracks into one package and attracts more than 350,000 fans annually. In addition to the 500-mile stock car race, Riverside hosts the U.S. Road Racing Championships for sports cars in May, the *Hot Rod* Magazine Championship Drag Races in April, the Los Angeles Times Grand Prix for sports cars in October and, on an every-other-year basis, the American Road Race of Champions to determine the national amateur sports car titles. November of 1967 saw the birth of a 300-mile USAC Championship race on one of the sports car courses.

Riverside added a 400-mile event for stock cars in 1970 which is known as the Falstaff 400 and is usually run in June. Richard Petty won the new event in 1970 and 1971.

The basic nine-turn course is 3.2 miles long and incorporates both right- and left-hand turns, including four 180-degree-angle turns. A second sports car course is 2.6 miles in length, eliminating two 180-degree turns in favor of two 90-degree turns. In addition to the two sports car courses, the layout includes a quarter-mile drag strip and a half-mile asphalt oval. The drag strip is the scene of regular Sunday events and the half-mile oval sees duty with late model stock cars, motorcycles and go-karts.

Major tire and accessory manufacturers make good use of the various facilities in their testing programs. Several television commercials and movies have been shot at the track. In addition, special driver courses are offered amateur race drivers to accustom them to the rigors of competition. The courses teach the basic preparation of a race car, handling characteristics at high speed, how to get around in traffic and other basic skills necessary in driving a race car.

The Stock Car Course

A 2.7-mile course incorporating both right- and left-hand turns and a series of esses comprises the layout that presents a special challenge to the southern stock car driver, who supposedly knows nothing but left-turn racing. The abrupt change from strictly left-turn racing has a tendency to cause problems as the southern drivers hit the two-way turn situation.

Despite this, David Pearson and former IMCA three-time

Jim Paschal demolished his Plymouth in the first annual Motor Trend 500 going over the guard rail, which has since been replaced by a retaining wall of boiler plate.

point champion Dick Hutcherson seem to have the track pretty well under control. Pearson set a new record in 1966 in his Dodge, and Hutcherson brought a 1967 Fairlane to Riverside and eclipsed Pearson's time to earn the pole position with a speed of 106.591 miles an hour.

Parnelli Jones holds the current qualifying record with a speed of 113.310 miles an hour set in 1970. Richard Petty owns the race records for both the 500- and 400-mile distances. Petty set the 500-mile mark in 1969 driving his Ford at an average speed of 105.498 miles an hour. In 1970 Petty returned in a Plymouth to establish a mark of 101.120 miles an hour for a 400-mile stock car race.

The start-finish line is near the south end of the course, and from the drop of the green flag there is absolutely no rest for the driver. A few hundred yards from the start drivers must make a 45-degree left turn and then another 45-degree turn back to the right. Then at about 115 miles an hour the cars proceed through the esses to turn six. Brakes must be applied and quick gear reductions made to prevent the car from hurtling off the north end of the track. The sharp right at turn six is followed by a short straight and gearing down to second for turn eight, a 180-degree reverse turn which leads into the back straight.

From second gear the cars accelerate to speeds approaching 160 miles an hour as they proceed down the mile-long straightaway with a slight dip near the Champion bridge, which crosses the backstretch with an overhead walkway. Deceleration at the end of the back straight leads into the most dangerous turn on the track—turn nine. It was here that Joe Weatherly was killed in 1964 when his car slammed into a retaining wall. At the very same spot Billy Foster of Victoria, British Columbia, was killed in 1967 during a practice run.

Out of turn nine the cars flash past the start-finish line and start around the course again. The pits are located near the south end of the track just where the cars come out of turn nine, making pit stops just a little easier, because of the reduced speeds.

Turn six has caused Fred Lorenzen no little trouble in his efforts to get around Riverside. In 1966 Lorenzen flipped his Galaxie there six times, demolishing the brand-new car. The wreck occurred so close to race time that Lorenzen was unable to compete. In 1967 Fred found turn six to be his nemesis again. He went to Riverside three weeks before the race to break in his Category II Fairlane with exhaustive testing. During the tests he broadsided through turn six and tore up the front suspension on his car. Repairs were made in time for race day.

Four-time winner Dan Gurney pushes his Wood Brothers-prepared 1966 Ford through the esses, making the tires smoke.

Four-time Winner Unseated

Of major interest to the stock car fan is the Motor Trend 500, which attracts one of the top fields of drivers, both oval and road racing. A purse of more than $85,000 helps draw road-racing drivers, who are more familiar with the course, to compete with top NASCAR drivers from the South.

As the first race of the year and the first event in which the newest model cars can compete, it is eagerly awaited by most stock car racing buffs. Although one man seems to have had the Motor Trend 500 in his hip pocket, there was always a great deal of interest in watching for someone to come along and beat Dan Gurney at what had jokingly been referred to as the "Gurney 500."

From the inauguration of the event in 1963 through the first four races, the California driver completely dominated the action. His experience on the course and a natural ability to push a car to the limit without breaking it have been cited as reasons for his consistent winning. There were some close calls, but Gurney, who developed the American Eagle and heads All American Racers, managed to outlast all comers.

David Pearson, eventual winner of the 1966 Grand National point championship, set a new one lap record of 106.078 miles an hour and finished a close second to Gurney in the 1966 race. Curtis Turner was the only man able to pass Gurney on the track after Gurney took over the lead from Pearson on the eighth lap. A series of slow pit stops cost Turner any chance of overtaking Gurney, but the four-time winner admitted that Turner was all the competition he wanted.

In 1967 it was a different story. Parnelli Jones parlayed a combination of car, preparation, pit crew and driving with the head instead of his foot to end Gurney's reign at Riverside. The Torrance, California, driver won the Los Angeles Times Grand Prix in 1964. He led the Motor Trend 500 by more than a lap in 1964 when his engine broke, and the former Indianapolis "500" winner was eliminated.

Ironically Jones used a portion of the Gurney formula to bring his 1967 Ford Fairlane home in front. His pit crew was the same one which had handled Gurney's car in three of his four previous wins—the Wood Brothers. Cale Yarborough was slated to drive the Wood car until the second day of time trials when he bashed the rear end in turn nine, and there was no way to repair the car in time for the race.

Jones was piloting a car built by Holman and Moody of

Parnelli Jones leads David Pearson through the esses at Riverside.

Curtis Turner found the going just a little rough in 1966 and spun off the course. He regained control and rejoined the race.

Charlotte and prepared by H-M's West Coast operation under Bill Stroppe. With Cale forced to sit it out, the Woods were asked to pit Jones' car. They did, and were part of the winning combination which brought a record purse of $21,980. Jones led for 126 of the 185 laps, taking over for the last time on lap 85 and leading the remainder of the race.

1967 Motor Trend 500

Parnelli averaged 91.08 miles an hour in the race, which was interrupted by rain and had to be called after 50 laps. A week later the competition was resumed. Fred Lorenzen had started his Holman-Moody Ford in the fifth spot and had worked his way up into first place when the rains came. When the southern California smog liquified to the point where continuing the race became impossible, Fred was in the pits to have a flat on the right rear fixed.

As the race was halted, NASCAR officials ordered the drivers and pit crews to leave the cars just as they were, and the pearl-white Ford had to sit there with a flat right rear tire. The following week the race was restarted under the caution flag, while Lorenzen sat impatiently in his car waiting for the other cars to cross the start-finish line before his pit crew could replace the rubber and fill his gas tank.

Parnelli Jones pulls in for a pit stop as Leonard Wood indicates where he's to stop. Note Glen Wood with one foot on the wall ready to go to work as soon as the car halts.

The flat tire proved very costly for Lorenzen, who dropped from first to 11th position before he could get back into action. The gritty driver worked his way back up to third place before his 396 CID engine gave up the ghost. But Lorenzen wasn't the only driver who had troubles. The favored Gurney blinked one time too many and missed a caution flag, passing Jones in a mad dash down pit road and out onto the course and back into the race.

The honest mistake cost Gurney a lap, and a slow pit stop for gas and rubber a few laps later proved even costlier as Jones amassed an insurmountable lead. Gurney's problems ended when his engine coughed up its insides all over the track, and the four-time winner watched an unprecedented fifth straight victory fly out the window.

Mechanical problems and wrecks claimed a major part of the field, with only 13 cars still able to move under their own power when the checkered flag fell. Lloyd Ruby, Mario Andretti and A. J. Foyt all joined Gurney in a cloud of 30-weight oil as they blew their engines. Pole-sitter Dick Hutcherson got in some heavy traffic in turn six and couldn't avoid another car. Curtis Turner, driving a Bud Moore 1967 Mercury Cyclone as a teammate of Gurney, also ran into heavy traffic in turn six and found himself in the pits watching the remainder of the race. Lee Roy Yarbrough managed to crunch the right side of his car during the early stages and then rolled over in turn two after the rains came.

David Pearson encountered one problem after another as the race wore on, going into the pits time after time. But he always came back out and managed to finish eighth. Cotton Owens, builder of Pearson's car, knew the driver was strong, but he almost fainted when Pearson pulled into the pits coming off turn nine with his gearshift lever in his hand.

Ford maintained its superiority with the first-place showing of Jones, but MoPar finished hard and strong behind him. Paul Goldsmith finished second in a Plymouth with Norm Nelson close behind in another Mayflower. Don White, runner-up in the 1966 USAC point championship, was fourth in a Dodge Charger and James Hylton, 1966 NASCAR Rookie of the Year, was fifth in a 1965 Dodge.

Gurney returned in 1968 to make it five out of six and continue Ford's domination. Richard Petty finally cracked victory circle on the twisting road course in 1969, but it happened to be the year he switched to Ford to make it seven straight victories for FoMoCo.

In 1970 A. J. Foyt, one of the world's foremost race drivers, extended Ford's win streak to eight.

Ray Elder is the only Western Grand National driver ever to capture the coveted checkered flag at Riverside and in so doing broke Ford's stronghold. Elder pushed his Dodge into victory circle over all of the top eastern drivers plus a number of international driving stars.

BRIDGEHAMPTON RACE CIRCUIT

The 2.85-mile Bridgehampton Race Circuit was the last road course on the East Coast to host NASCAR Grand National stock car events. Set in the picturesque, gently rolling Long Island countryside, the twisting, hilly course offered the stockers the only right- and left-hand-turn challenge outside of Riverside.

Watkin's Glen hosted a 150-mile event until 1966. Marvin Panch captured the 1965 race at the Glen, pushing his Wood Brothers' Ford around the 2.3-mile course at an average speed of better than 98 miles an hour. When Watkin's Glen dropped its NASCAR-sanctioned GN event, the Bridgehampton promoters continued to put a little variety into their sports car dominated schedule. The stock car race was scheduled as a part of the annual Grand National northern tour, usually early in July.

169

Track History

While the present paved closed circuit only dates back to 1957, the racing era at Bridgehampton goes all the way back to 1915. That year the finale of the annual Fireman's Fair held at the small farming village was a 15-mile road race. It was a smashing success, and for the next five years Essex, Chevrolet and Ford cars thundered through the village in hub-to-hub battles which had residents buzzing for months before and after.

By 1920 the annual event had grown to a 50-mile run. Then there was a hiatus until 1949 when the roar of unmuffled engines reverberated over the potato fields and through the quiet vacation resort to start another five-year reign of racing as king.

The races staged June 11, 1949, were over a four-mile course of public roads. The course was rectangular with four major corners, a few quick bends, a few hills (including one ridge which lifted the cars a foot off the ground at high speed) and the long concrete straight Ocean Road.

From 1949 through the final race run over public roads in 1953, the crowds swelled from a few area residents to more than 40,000. Known as the "round the houses event," the race offered all the thrills of the highly touted European races.

Crowd control was becoming a major problem for the farming hamlet of less than 2,000. Robert Wilder was killed May 22, 1953, when his car flipped during practice. The Town Board held an emergency session at which the final decision was to permit the races to continue, provided there were no more accidents. The next day there were two major accidents. One involved only a car and driver, but the second saw Harry Grey roll a Jag at 100 miles an hour into a crowd standing in a prohibited area.

The Town Board didn't have to halt the race, because thousands of milling fans jammed the course, making racing impossible. The short-lived romance with big-time racing entered a four-year period of hibernation. Westhampton Air Force Base hosted racing during the interim, but local enthusiasts weren't satisfied.

The unlikely combination of a garage owner, a state highway patrolman and a printer pushed the idea of a closed course to insure crowd control and accomplished the almost impossible task of raising $300,000 for land, grading, paving and other necessities.

The result is one of the world's top closed-circuit race tracks. But the problems didn't end with building the track. Sunday "blue laws" forbade auto racing. Local townspeople relented eventually,

170

A closely packed group of Grand National cars negotiate a right-hand turn at Bridgehampton.

and the blue laws were repealed. Other legal hassles, bad weather, erosion and poor attendance during the initial events plagued the track during its first few seasons. Events were added and expanded. Facilities have been improved, and the profits are being poured back into the physical plant, resulting in an up-to-date race circuit.

Track Layout

The course consists of 2.85 miles of tortuous, twisting hills and downgrades with nine turns, of which one is a tight hairpin. The track is 30 feet wide except in front of the pits where it widens to 50 feet. Two long straights give the cars plenty of running room and a chance to let it all out. The east straight is 2,125 feet long, and the pit straight, passing the start-finish line, measures 3,100 feet.

Going into the first turn, the drivers come off the end of the pit straightaway into a right-hand downgrade turn. Through the second and third turns the cars continue downhill. Coming out of the 90-degree fourth turn, the cars start a steep climb as they set up for the first of two left-hand bends. Along the back straight the cars run down through the seventh turn before reaching the 180-degree hairpin turn. From the hairpin the cars must accelerate

David Pearson leads the cars through a tortuous turn at Bridgehampton.

Down the pit straight and past the start-finish line winner David Pearson leads the field.

uphill along the east straight, make a 90-degree right-hand turn and then start down the main chute to begin all over again.

The elevation ranges from 132 feet above sea level in the hairpin to a high of 265 feet at the start-finish line. Carved out of a near wilderness, the circuit offers a panoramic view of Peconic Bay in the distance. Sand and scrub oak dominate the low areas. Stands are sparse, but there is plenty of room in the infield. With the variation in topography, the vantage points are good.

1966 Bridgehampton 150

The 1966 Grand National point champion, David Pearson, had a relatively easy time in winning the 1966 event. He finished almost a full lap in front of James Hylton, who was runner-up to Pearson in the point battle.

During the 10-lap qualifying race, Richard Petty's hemi-hummer seemed to be the only car in the field of 28 that could offer Pearson's 1965 Dodge any real competition. However, Petty burned out a main bearing in that race and wasn't able to replace his engine in time for the feature event. Pearson's victory saw only 18 cars still running at the finish, mechanical failures having left the others by the wayside.

The Grand National point champion's success on road courses belongs, at least in part, to the factory representative who delivered a car with a four-speed manual transmission to the veteran driver. The car arrived in October of 1965, and until the practice sessions got underway at Riverside three months later, David couldn't understand why the four-speed box. Finishing second to Dan Gurney's Ford in the Motor Trend 500 was a big thrill for the veteran, and he was quick to admit that the extra three months of practice in shifting hadn't hurt any. Pearson showed that it must have been of some help when he walked away with the only other road-course event on the NASCAR schedule.

Bridgehampton was a demanding course for stockers due to the constant shifting—a strange experience for the NASCAR drivers who usually only change gears coming out of the pits and then run flat out. This shifting caused many transmission failures.

Just over 5,000 fans were on hand to witness the hairy full-size cars on the tight road course. Some observers complained that the stockers made little effort to get set up for the right-left situations, but one NASCAR driver pointed out that it required several full days' work to make the changeover from the all-left-turn courses.

Another driver said that only one of the northern tour events was on a road course while the others were strictly left-hand turns over closed ovals. He hinted that longer races with larger purses and more prestige would help convince NASCAR drivers to make efforts similar to those expended to win at Riverside.

The Grand National races at Bridgehampton have been replaced by 300-mile events scheduled at Trenton Speedway in Trenton, New Jersey in July and at Dover Speedway in Dover, Delaware in October. The last race at Bridgehampton was in 1966.

GLOSSARY

Accessory award—Prize money added to the normal purse by manufacturers.

AHRA—American Hot Rod Association. Sanctioning body for drag racing.

Apron—Low, flat edge of race track used in case of emergency.

ARCA—Automobile Racing Club of America.

Baldies—Tires whose tread surface has no grooves.

Binders—Brakes.

Bite—Traction on a race track.

Blown engine—When some part of engine breaks causing a puff of smoke.

Bonnet—Crash helmet.

Bottom out—Suspension compressed to the limit of its travel by centrifugal force on car as it enters high-bank turn on high-speed run.

Broadslide—Driving sideways through turn on dirt track.

Charger—Go-or-blow driver; runs at maximum speed all the time.

Chief mechanic—The "Boss" of racing operations.

Chopping—Cutting in front of rival car.

Chute—Fast part of race track in front of main grandstand.

Clean—Well-built car. (Also referred to as "Sanitary.")

Closed track—Any track generally circular in shape.

Clunker—Sluggish, beat-up car.

Come apart—When engine blows and sprays metal on the track.

Corner—Curve on oval race track.

Crew chief—Mechanic in charge of pit operations.

Cross-up—When one car slides sideways out of control.

Dirt dobber—Driver who would prefer to race on dirt tracks.

Dirt tracking—Controlled power slide. Term usually used for driver using dirt track driving techniques on paved track.

Dogging—Driving extremely close behind another car in effort to force a mistake.

Drafting—Method used at super-speedways to obtain faster speed and conserve fuel. One car will drive close on bumper of another, creating a vacuum in draft so both cars will go faster due to less turbulence and wind resistance.

Drag race—A test of acceleration over a very short distance, usually a quarter of a mile.

Drag tires—Tires designed solely and specifically for drag racing.

Factory team—Drivers and mechanics who receive some form of subsistence from Detroit manufacturers.

175

Fastback—Car with sloping back.

Featherfoot—Very cautious driver.

FIA—Federation Internationale de l'Automobile—The sole international sanctioning body entitled to make and enforce rules and regulations for the encouragement and control of automobile competitions.

Flat-out—Fast as machine will run.

FoMoCo—Ford Motor Company products.

Gasoline alley—Garage area of speedways.

Goat—A Dodge.

Grand National—Late Model stock car circuit.

Groove—That part of the race track where cars handle best at peak speeds.

Hairy—Tension when cars are running close together and hard to handle.

Handling—Car's chassis performance.

Hanging it out—Swerving rear end extremely to make car resemble power slide on major speedway.

Hemi—Engine equipped with hemispherical-shaped combustion chamber.

Hemi-hummer—A Plymouth or a Dodge.

Henry—A Ford.

High riser—Manifold which puts carburetor higher over engine for better performance from improved gas flow.

Hit the binders—Put on brakes.

Honking—Running exceptionally well.

Hot dog—Leading driver on one of various circuits. Ex.: "He's a Grand National Hot Dog."

IMCA—International Motor Contest Association.

Infield—Area enclosed by oval track.

Knobbies—Tires with rough tread, similar to old-style snow tires.

Late model—Race car no more than three years old.

Laying the iron on—When a driver gets inside another on track and bumps against him in order to hold traction and get by.

Leaning on him—When one driver gets inside another and lets him know he's there by crowding the turns.

Leadfoot—Driver who keeps accelerator on or near floor.

Lets go—When something breaks.

Loop her—When driver spins out. This term more commonly used when driver deliberately spins car to avoid a wreck.

Lose it–When a driver loses control of his car.

Lunch—Destroy an engine.

Major speedway—Track of one mile or more in length which stages races of major proportion in length and purse. Superspeedway.

Mayflower—A Plymouth.

Money grabber—Driver who starts race and quits after minimum number of laps to pick up easy money just for entering and starting.

MoPar—Chrysler products (Dodge and Plymouth).

Motor mouth—Someone in the pits who talks a lot.

NASCAR—National Association for Stock Car Auto Racing, world's largest stock car race sanctioning body.

NHRA—National Hot Rod Association. Sanctioning body for drag racing.

Pace car—Car that leads pack through one or two laps just before race starts. Pace car also paces race under caution flag.

Pacer—Steady, consistent driver.

Parade lap—Ceremonial lap made by lined-up cars before pace lap and race.

Pits—Trackside area accommodating repair crew of each driver.

Pit crew—The team of mechanics who work on a race car and service it during race.

176

Pole position—Coveted front inside spot given driver with best qualifying speed.

Pony—A Pontiac.

Pushing—When front end of car has tendency to drift to outside.

Rag—A poorly built, poorly painted car.

Ragtop—A convertible.

Ride—Opportunity to drive a car in a race.

Roll bar—Hollow steel tubing that forms an arch over the driver's head to protect him in case his car rolls over.

Roll cage—A complete network of roll bars and connecting braces that provide increased protection to the driver.

Running scared—Performance of driver scared by recent accident.

Sanitary—In top racing condition.

Shaky—A Chevrolet.

Shoes—Race tires.

Skins—Tires.

Slingshot—Method used to pass on high-speed tracks. Trailing car moves out of draft of leader, creating a vacuum which then pulls front car back.

Soup-up—Change or modify engine to increase speed.

Spoiler—Device used to improve a car's handling at high speed.

Stand on it—Push accelerator to floor and leave it there.

Stroker—Driver who keeps steady pace.

Stovebolt—A Chevrolet.

Sway bar—Suspension component designed to improve handling.

Tach—Short for tachometer.

Tough—Something nice.

Toy—A race car.

USAC—United States Auto Club—sanctioning body for championship car races as well as sprints and stocks.

Wedge—Raise or lower various corners of race car to shift weight and improve handling.

Yellow bumper—Rear bumper of cars driven by first-year drivers on NASCAR tracks are painted yellow to warn veterans they are behind inexperienced competitors. Ex.: "He's a yellow bumper."

INDEX

A

Acton, Marv, 46
Alameda, Cal., 98
Allison, Bobby, 42–44, 46, 54, 82, 120, 126, 127, 141, 143, 144, 150, 151, 153, 154, 155, 156–157
Allison, Donnie, 42–44, 83, 84, 126–127, 143, 144, 146
Amick, Bill, 100, 103
Andretti, Mario, 120, 123, 168
Andrews, Wayne, 68
Antioch, Cal., see Tracks, paved
Asheville, N.C., see Tracks, paved
Atascadero, Cal., see Tracks, paved
Atlanta, Ga., see Tracks, super-speedways
Augusta, Ga., see Tracks, paved

B

Baker, Buck, 41, 52, 68, 72, 91, 106, 112–113, 161
Baker, Buddy, 42, 48, 120, 127, 143, 144
Ballard, Walter, 46
Balmer, Earl, 111, 122
Barkheimer, Bob, 98, 103
Baton Rouge, La., see Tracks, paved
Batteries, 21–22, 88
Bay Cities Racing Association, 98
Bealessio, Steve, 103
Beauchamp, Johnny, 117
Beltsville, Md., see Tracks, paved
Bergman, Carl S., see Stevens, Bugs
Birmingham, Ala., see Tracks, paved
Bodies, 17, 31, 33, 80, 88
Boggs, David, 68
Brakes, 21
Brasington, Harold, 134
Brickhouse, Richard, 143

Bridgehampton, N.Y., see Tracks, road courses
Bristol, Tenn., see Tracks, paved
Brown, Perk, 83, 85, 86, 91, 150
Brown, Richard, 46
Bumpers, 21, 88, 93
Burdick, Bob, 132
Burgess, Grafton, 153
Burris, Carl, 83, 91
Byron, Red, 82, 84, 105, 148

C

Cadet Class, 70, 94–95, 96
Cagel, Red, 12
Cain, Scotty, 102
California Stock Car Racing Association, 98, 99
Campbell, Sir Malcolm, 113
Campbell, Wally, 105
Camshafts, 35, 81, 94
Carburetors, 22, 35, 66, 72, 80, 87, 93, 94
CARS (makes and models)
  Barracuda, 65
  Belvedere, 17
  Buick, 105
  Cadillac, 79, 105
  Camaro, 65, 68
  Challenger, 65
  Charger, 9, 17, 35, 36, 101–102, 122, 123, 169
  Chevelle, 121, 150, 154
  Chevrolet, 11, 73, 74, 79, 83, 88, 94, 128, 170
  Chrysler, 13, 22, 41, 135, 138
  Comet, 112, 151
  Coronet, 9, 17
  Cougar, 65, 68
  Cyclone, 168
  Dart, 65